Palgrave Studies on Global Poli
Futures in Education

Series Editors
Michael Thomas
Liverpool John Moores University
Liverpool, UK

Jeffrey R. Di Leo
University of Houston-Victoria
Victoria, TX, USA

This transdisciplinary series investigates developments in the field of education in the age of neoliberalism, interrogating arguments and evidence for and against it as well as envisioning alternative educational futures. While much has been written about neoliberalism a key aim of the series is to explore and develop critical perspectives on how neoliberal and corporatist approaches have changed and impacted on educational institutions across all sectors, from schools to higher education, across the globe. The series engages with academics, researchers, curriculum developers, teachers, students and policy makers and provokes them to consider how neoliberal trends and values are affecting the direction of our educational institutions. Comparative studies with the US in particular as well as other prominent national and international contexts that have promoted these values will be encouraged alongside the UK, Australia and EU to identify the implications of recent policies, strategies and values on teaching, learning and research. Posing important questions and developing a critique around the need for evidence lies at the center of the series, which invites responses from advocates and proponents alike in order to shape an agenda which looks forward to making an impact on policy making. The series brings together a critical mass of evidence and aims to foster critical understanding and to understand the influence of neoliberal thinking on education in order to articulate alternative futures at this crucial moment when many professionals are deeply concerned about the developments taking place.

To submit a proposal, please contact the editors or commissioning editor:

Michael Thomas: m.thomas@ljmu.ac.uk and Jeffrey R. Di Leo: dileo@symploke.org

Milana Vernikova: Commissioning Editor, milana.vernikova@palgrave-usa.com

More information about this series at
http://www.palgrave.com/gp/series/16341

Ewan Ingleby

Neoliberalism Across Education

Policy And Practice From Early Childhood
Through Adult Learning

Ewan Ingleby
Middlesbrough, UK

Palgrave Studies on Global Policy and Critical Futures in Education
ISBN 978-3-030-73964-5   ISBN 978-3-030-73962-1   (eBook)
https://doi.org/10.1007/978-3-030-73962-1

Cover illustration: © Sally Anderson / Alamy

This Palgrave Pivot imprint is published by the registered company Springer Nature Switzerland AG.
The registered company address is: Gewerbestrasse 11, 6330 Cham, Switzerland

ACKNOWLEDGEMENTS

Thank you to Professor Michael Thomas for inviting me to be part of this monograph series. The book is based on over 14 years of research into education in various contexts. I am also grateful to my friends and colleagues in education, (Dr Clive Hedges [Teesside University], Dr Jonathan Tummons [Durham University], and Dr Barbara Wilford [Teesside University]) who have contributed in direct and indirect ways to the conversations about research in education that have helped to fashion the content of this book.

I wish to dedicate the book to my father who died in March 2017. My dad was very much a wordsmith and he would have been intrigued and amused by the words in this book. I can almost hear him saying with incredulity: 'simulacra!? You can't be serious!'. However, my dad would have been interested in this book, and he would also have been delighted that my daughter Teresa is currently reading English Language and Literature at Hertford College, Oxford. As ever, I am particularly grateful to my wife Karen and my children Bernadette, Teresa, and Michael. Without them, tomorrow would always be a much harder day.

Dr Ewan Ingleby, November 2020.

CONTENTS

CHAPTER 1

Introduction

A neoliberal conceptualisation of society links to the writing of Friedman and Friedman (1980) and Hayek (1976). Olssen et al. (2004) argue that the philosophical background of this approach to policy-making connects with Hume, Ricardo and Smith. At the centre of these philosophies is a belief in competitive individualism and the maximisation of the market (Saunders 2010, 42). Löwith (1993, 19) argues that in helping us to understand what neoliberalism is, the Weberian image of the destruction of a magic garden of faith and certainty and its replacement with an apocalyptic vision of a rational world of measurement is a helpful way of understanding neoliberalism. The implication is that we witness a fundamental unhappiness in the attempts that are made to quantify and measure the social world in what are referred to as neoliberal societies. The economic essence of neoliberalism and its consequences for social policies has been commented on by critics including Apple (2001), Giroux (2000, 2005), Harvey (2005) and Torres (1998, 2008). These academics argue that the emphasis that is given to economic outcomes in neoliberal societies produces particular consequences for social, political, cultural, and educational institutions.

E. Ingleby, *Neoliberalism Across Education*, Palgrave Studies on Global Policy and Critical Futures in Education, https://doi.org/10.1007/978-3-030-73962-1_1

In this book I reflect on the impact of neoliberalism on education in England. There are six key chapters, and the first main chapter explores the impact that neoliberalism has had on early years education (with children aged from birth to eight years of age) with technology. In the second main chapter, the consequences of emphasising the importance of educational results for primary and secondary schools in England are explored. Chapter 4 focuses on the political and economic processes that have created academy schools in England and the unforeseen consequences this has had for the English FE (Further Education) context. Chapter 5 reflects on the impact that neoliberalism has had on the FE sector in England by presenting research findings on the emergence of mentoring in FE. I argue that the influence of Ofsted (The Office for Standards in Education) has resulted in the emergence of a mentoring model that is judgemental of teaching ability and not necessarily supportive and developmental. In Chap. 6, HE in FE (Higher Education in Further Education) is explored. It is argued that the policy documents that have created HE in FE (for example BIS [The Department for Business, Innovation and Skills] 2009, 2013; DfES [The Department for Education and Skills] 2003; The Browne Report 2010) have underestimated the complexity of the higher education sector and that interventions have occurred that have produced detrimental consequences for students in England. The final main chapter explores professional development in education under neoliberalism. It is argued that there are few examples of what Kennedy (2005) refers to as a full sense of transformative professional development due to the emphasis that is placed on achieving successful examination results.

The Educational Context

This book is being written at a time when there are acute financial pressures in schools in England as a consequence of neoliberalism. A combined survey by the ATL (the Association of Teachers and Lecturers) and the NUT (the National Teachers Union) in 2017 identified that funding pressures in England have led to schools resorting to new ways of raising money and in consequence the professional development of educators is not a priority area. The research findings from the ATL (2017) reveal that although support-staff in schools consider that they do work that is identical to teaching staff; they are not enabled by CPD (Continuing Professional Development) to develop this form of pedagogy. The financial pressures that the schools are experiencing do not appear to equip them with the resources that are necessary to meet professional development needs. The survey revealed that 44% of schools rent out school buildings and that one-sixth of schools are asking the parents of students for money to help with school finances (ATL 2017). I argue that transformative professional development is less likely to happen because of these funding pressures. In the survey of 1200 teachers, support staff, and heads, 76% of the staff revealed that their budgets had been cut in 2017, and 93% of the respondents claimed to be pessimistic about the prospects for their school's funding over the subsequent three years from 2017. Moreover, 71% of the secondary school respondents revealed that their school had cut teaching posts and 50% of the total number of respondents noted that they have had to increase class sizes. The survey also shows that 41% of schools have had to cut their SEN (Special Educational Needs) provision and that the opportunities for professional development in this specialist area of education have been reduced. The statements by the respondents reveal the challenges that exist for educators in schools in England. In the survey, a primary teacher from Essex in England reflected that the school ethos in general is preventing opportunities for effective professional development (ATL 2017).

The ATL and the NUT (2017) research makes reference to the pedagogical occurrence of a teacher having to teach a master class of 64 pupils with no developmental support (ATL 2017). According to the survey, schools are being forced to go to increasing lengths to raise money to cope with funding shortfalls in England and this is preventing the development of CPD opportunities. Almost half (49%) of the respondents reported that their school had asked parents to pay for items to help their child's education, including textbooks and art and design materials, so the possibility of financing and enabling what Kennedy (2005) phrases as transformative CPD is less likely (ATL 2017). 14 of these respondents said that their school asks parents for over £20 a month. The survey was published on the first day of the ATL's annual conference in Liverpool, in April 2017, where five motions on the subject of school funding and its associated consequences were debated. Mary Bousted, the ATL's general secretary, warned of the severely limited choices that exist for schools and the associated professional development of educators (ATL 2017). Kevin Courtney, from the NUT, criticised the English Conservative government's approach to education and CPD by pleading for the government to invest in education for the sake of its children and its educators (ATL 2017).

The challenges to school funding appear to be part of the broader context of educational flux in schools in England. I argue that this relates to a series of neoliberal educational policies that have been made by governments in England since 2010 (Selwyn 2011, cited in Ingleby 2015a). These policies have included reforming the examination system and diversifying the forms of schools in England (Ingleby 2015a). It can be argued that the intervention by governments in England in the primary and secondary school system since 2010 is framed by a background of the aim of achieving financial efficiency (Machin and Vernoit 2011). In this policy approach, the effective professional development of educators in schools has not been fully considered, and its characteristics can be summarised as equating to 'an ambition of absence' (Selwyn 2011, 365, cited in Ingleby 2015a). As opposed to championing the merits of aligning the schools to governmental control so that the CPD needs of the educators are met, the approach that has been favoured by English governments since 2010, is to encourage autonomy and self- regulation (Machin and Vernoit 2011). The ideal position that the governments in England have encouraged since 2010, is for the schools to manage their affairs in 'independent' ways that are 'outside the control of local authorities' (Machin and Vernoit 2011, 2). In consequence, the professional development needs of educators are not being met. The academics who have explored the implications of this policy approach include Clarke (2014) who reflects on the potentially unsettling consequences this has for schools' organisation, and Ball (2010) who argues that policies and practice in schools in England are not aligned together effectively. Caldwell and Harris (2008) argue that schools can produce the 'transformation' that Kennedy (2005) references, however, this is crucially linked to adequate resourcing and finance. There appear to be other critical factors that are influencing educators in contemporary England. These factors include a preoccupation with educational results (Glatter 2012); the conflicts of interest that can become apparent between stakeholders in schools (Greany and Scott 2014); the interpretation of educational leadership that is given by neoliberal politicians (Gunter 2011); alongside the perceived priorities of state education (Hatcher 2011). Moreover, within educational contexts in England there are differing interpretations of quality (Machin and Salvanes 2010); and differing understandings over what constitutes best practice with regards to institutional governance (McCrone et al. 2011). In other words, a complex set of circumstances are shaping educational contexts in England as a consequence of neoliberalism. It is also argued by Urban (2009) that there is an absence of educational philosophy across the sector and that there exists a void that is filled with initiatives that are based on neoliberal political and socio-economic imperatives. This reveals a number of key characteristics that apply to the research context.

THE CHAPTERS

The book is divided into six main chapters that consider and reflect on key neoliberal interventions in education in England across an educational spectrum that ranges from early years (children aged from birth to eight years), to primary, secondary, tertiary/further, and higher education. Alongside the application of theories (including the work of Barton [2007]; Baudrillard [1983, 1993]; Bernstein [2000]; Gee [1996]) there is the application of primary and secondary research data to shed light on the consequences of neoliberalism for education in contemporary England. This data has been gathered by the author during a series of educational research projects in England from 2006–2018. Although this research has occurred in England, the book is relevant for an international audience as there are related themes linking to neoliberalism that are explored in other cultural contexts (for example, by Colmer et al. [2015] in Australia; Ilham et al. [2015] in the United States of America; Marklund [2015] in Sweden). It is argued by Ingleby (2015b) that neoliberal forms of government have consequences for education in a number of countries in the European Union, America and Australasia. This makes the book relevant for future research into education in neoliberal contexts.

The first main chapter investigates the application of technology to pedagogy in the early years. The content considers the perceptions of technology that are held by a variety of practitioners in a range of settings. The chapter explores the factors influencing the interpretation of the pedagogical value of technology by asking two questions. Do the educators follow neoliberal policymakers who support the application of technology to pedagogy? Do the educators mirror academic research in this area by considering that 'e is only best' when it is applied to pedagogy to develop creative thinking? The chapter draws on the experiences of practitioners who are working in either private or statutory nursery settings. The chapter reveals that a range of personal, social and professional factors influence educators' pedagogy with technology.

This first main chapter is followed by a reflection that builds on the research that was presented by Vermunt (2016) at the IPDA (International

Professional Development Association) conference by arguing that we need to listen to conversations in learning spaces about schools and their organisational culture if we are to enable the successful development of school education. The theoretical framework of the chapter is based on the work of Bernstein (2000) as a means of advancing knowledge as to why schools in England prioritise academic results over a full sense of creative education. The chapter presents key elements of schools' organisational culture in England that have been shaped by neoliberalism. The content considers the consequences that this has for the pedagogy that is occurring in primary and secondary schools in England.

Chapter 4 explores the consequences of the introduction of academy schools in England for FE. It is argued that the uncertainty of the remit of academy schools has indirect consequences for FE and that the employability agenda of the sector is challenged by academy schools. This appears to be happening because of years of neoliberal government neglect of the FE sector in England. The chapter applies the work of the French philosopher Jean Baudrillard (1983, 1993) by arguing that the academy schools are simulating the FE agenda. In simulation, a model of reality precedes what is real. The uncertainty surrounding the exact purpose of the academy schools appears to enable them to adopt agendas that have been traditionally associated with other sectors of education. This original argument forms the basis of the new knowledge in the chapter.

In Chap. 5, consideration is given to the competing understandings of mentoring that are present within the FE sector in England. The Anderson and Shannon (1988) model of mentoring is based on a nurturing, caring, Rogerian philosophy, however, this contrasts with other mentoring models (for example Daloz 1986) that are favoured by neoliberal governments and combine 'support' with 'challenge'. This latter judgemental model of mentoring can be used to assess the effectiveness of the educators' ability to teach and it appears to be the preferred choice of Ofsted (Office for Standards in Education) (Lawy and Tedder 2011). The chapter considers the consequences that this choice of mentoring model is having for the FE sector in England and introduces the theoretical concept of literacy as social practice that is explored and applied in the subsequent chapters of the book. Drawing on the work of Barton (2007), and Gee (1996), it is argued that education In England under neoliberalism is shaped by 'literary texts' (for example neoliberal education policies), 'curriculum events' that are generated by educators in consequence of these texts, and subjective 'practices' that constitute individual interpretations of these curriculum events.

The next main chapter is about HE in FE in England. The content reflects on the nature of this form of higher education in England. The policymakers ideally wish to see higher education leading to vocational expertise and employability. The chapter explores whether or not the perceptions of the policymakers are shared by the academics and students who work in HE in FE. The chapter reveals that although some of the academics and students reflect some of the views of the policymakers, other interpretations of HE in FE are present that differ from the policy documents. The chapter also interprets this educational context according to a theoretical framework that is based on interpreting theories of literacy as social practice and it is argued that this enables the content to make an original contribution in knowledge to an under-researched form of higher education in England.

Chapter 7 explores the perceptions of professional development that are held by educators in England. It is argued that there are few examples of what Kennedy (2005) refers to as 'transformative professional development' due to the emphasis that is placed on achieving successful examination results. This chapter is also developed via a theoretical background of literacy as social practice. It is argued that the 'texts' informing professional development (neoliberal policy documents and their recommendations) result in CPD 'events' and 'activities'. The chapter explores the personal subjective experiences (or 'practices') of CPD experienced by educators and considers the implications for professional development in education.

REFLECTION

Although often seemingly motivated by humanistic concerns, the discourse around neoliberalism has clear moralistic undertones, not least regarding the children and the parents of those involved in education. Simmons (2010, 369) argues that policy-making processes in key global societies like the USA and the UK are based on a number of basic assumptions about the nature of people and the role of the state. It is assumed that there are innate differences between individuals with respect to intelligence, motivation and moral character (Ingleby 2013). These assumed differences are the justification for interventions that supposedly foster a meritocracy and promote private ownership of previously public or communal resources, greater competition between providers (at least in the initial stages of private ownership) and the reification of 'market forces'; increasingly integral features of the dominant forms of both economic organisation and public discourse (Lauder et al. 2006, 25, cited in Ingleby 2013). As noted earlier, this conceptualisation of society is self-consciously based on the writing of Friedman and Friedman (1980) and Hayek (1976). However, as again noted, Olssen et al. (2004) argue that the philosophical background to this approach to policy-making connects further back, especially to a particular reading of Adam Smith. In Smith's (1991) case, this is not a straightforward reading as there are numerous examples of his support for state intervention to ensure the smooth functioning of society, particularly in relation to education (for example Smith, Book 5, Chapter 1, Part 3, Article 2). However, at the centre of these philosophies is a belief in competitive individualism and the maximisation of the market based on a fundamentally European Enlightenment and contractarian conception of social relations (Saunders 2010). The economic essence of neoliberalism aims to produce particular consequences for social, political, cultural and educational institutions. Mayo (2013) argues, for example, that the use of the word 'competences' is now a dominant discourse in neoliberal states so that the social world can be in turn 'measured', and that this will enable the shifting rewards of the global marketplace to be bestowed on competitive nations (Archer and Leathwood 2003). This association of 'competences' with 'measurement' results in 'school readiness' and 'employability' being woven together so that child and family rights become peripheral to education and employment (Ingleby 2013). In other words, the focus is not on the rights of the learner, but instead with a pre-determined set of criteria deemed to somehow serve future national economic interests (Ingleby 2013). However, I argue that in the logic of the discourse there is an elision between the sovereign individual and the sovereign nation.

The dominance of modes of discourse occurs due to complex global political and socio-economic processes and, like all hegemonic processes, they are only ever partial and contested, however their influence on discourse, academic as well as public, is still striking. Harris and Islar (2013) argue that these complex political and socio-economic processes are articulated through historical and political discourses where previous and current interpretations of society are used to generate a new understanding or synthesis of the social world. In view of the presence of this dominant discourse' I argue in this book that the problems that are evident in education will continue to be perpetuated and may, in fact, increase. Current policy is based on the primacy of capital accumulation and its pursuit in all its forms. This accumulation may not depend upon education *per se*, and whether or not it is beneficial to economic development is still a moot point. Contractarianism, of which neoliberalism is the dominant contemporary variant, inevitably serves to position the agent within a world based around the contract and, in particular, the employment contract, subordinating other social needs to this relationship, a relationship that is both social and anti-social at the same time. In this neoliberal world, children are regarded as having lesser interests because they cannot themselves uphold their rights. I argue that the possible solutions to the challenges in education that are revealed in this book cannot be realised until there exists a new synthesis of the purpose of the human world, and one that places the interests of education at its heart as opposed to its margins.

REFERENCES

Anderson, E.M., and A. Shannon. 1988. Towards a conceptualisation of mentoring. *Journal of Teacher Education* 39 (1): 38–42.

Apple, M. 2001. Comparing neo-liberal projects and inequality in education. *Comparative Education* 37 (4): 409–423.

Archer, L., and C. Leathwood. 2003. Identities and inequalities in higher education. In *Higher education and social class: Issues of exclusion and inclusion*, ed. L. Archer, M. Hutchings, and A. Ross, 176–191. London: Routledge Falmer.

Association of Teachers and Lecturers (ATL). 2017. Accessed October 3, 2018. https://www.atl.org.uk/latest/atl-survey-finds-support-staff-increasingly-having-teach-lessons.

Ball, S. 2010. New class inequalities in education. Why education policy may be looking in the wrong place! Education policy, civil society and social class. *International Journal of Sociology and Social Policy* 30 (3–4): 155–166.

Barton, D. 2007. *Literacy: An introduction to the ecology of written language.* Oxford: Blackwell Publishing.

Baudrillard, J. 1983. *Simulations.* London: MIT Press.

———. 1993. *Symbolic exchange and death.* London: Sage.

Bernstein, B. 2000. *Pedagogy, symbolic control and identity.* Lanham, MD: Rowman and Littlefield.

Browne, J. 2010. *Securing a sustainable suture for higher education: An independent review of higher education funding and student finance.* London: UK Government.

Caldwell, B.J., and J. Harris. 2008. *Why not the best schools?* Camberwell: Acer Press.

Clarke, P. 2014. *Report into allegations concerning Birmingham schools arising from 'Trojan Horse' letter*. London: HMSO.

Colmer, K., M. Waniganayake, and L. Field. 2015. Implementing curriculum reform: Insights into how Australian early childhood directors view professional development and learning. *Professional Development in Education* 41 (2): 203–221.

Daloz, J. 1986. *Effective mentoring and teaching*. San Francisco: Jossey Bass.

Department for Business Innovation and Skills. 2009. *Higher ambitions: The future of universities in a knowledge economy*. Norwich: HMSO.

———. 2013. *Widening participation in higher education*. London: HMSO.

Department for Education and Skills. 2003. *The future of higher education*. Norwich: HMSO.

Friedman, M., and R.D. Friedman. 1980. *Free to choose*. London: Penguin.

Gee, J.P. 1996. *Social linguistics and literacies*. London: Routledge Falmer.

Giroux, H. 2000. *Impure acts*. London: Taylor and Francis.

———. 2005. *The terror of neo-liberalism: Cultural politics and the promise of democracy*. Boulder, CO: Paradigm Publishers.

Glatter, R. 2012. Persistent preoccupations: The rise and rise of school accountability in England. *Educational Management Administration and Leadership* 40 (5): 559–575.

Greany, T., and J. Scott. 2014. *Conflicts of interest in academy sponsorship arrangements. A report for the education select committee*. London: Institute of Education.

Gunter, H. 2011. *Leadership and the reform of education*. Bristol: Policy Press.

Harris, L., and M. Islar. 2013. Neoliberalism nature and changing modalities of environmental governance in contemporary Turkey. In *Global economic crisis and the politics of diversity*, ed. Y. Atasoy, 52–78. London: Palgrave Macmillan.

Harvey, D. 2005. *A brief history of neo-liberalism*. Oxford: Oxford University Press.

Hatcher, R. 2011. Local government against local democracy: A case study. In *The state and education policy: The academy programme*, ed. H. Gunter, 39–52. London: Bloomsbury.

Hayek, F. 1976. *Law, legislation and liberty, vol. 2*. London: Routledge and Kegan Paul.

Ilham, N., J.K. Kidd, M.S. Burns, and T. Campbell. 2015. Head start classroom teachers' and assistant teachers' perception of professional development using a LEARN framework. *Professional Development in Education* 41 (2): 344–365.

Ingleby, E. 2013. Teaching policy and practice: Early years, neoliberalism and communities of practice. *Contemporary social science* 8 (2): 120–129.

———. 2015a. The impact of changing policies about technology on the professional development needs of early years educators in England. *Professional Development in Education* 41 (1): 144–158.

———. 2015b. The house that Jack built: Neoliberalism, teaching in higher education and the moral objections. *Teaching in Higher Education* 20 (5): 507–518.

Kennedy, A. 2005. Models of CPD: A framework for analysis. *Journal of In-service Education* 31 (2): 235–250.

Lauder, H., P. Brown, J. Dillabough, and A.H. Halsey. 2006. The prospects for education: Individualisation, globalisation and social change. In *Education globalisation and social change*, ed. H. Lauder, P. Brown, J. Dillabough, and A.H. Halsey, 1–70. Oxford: Oxford University Press.

Lawy, R., and M. Tedder. 2011. Mentoring and individual learning plans: Issues of practice in a period of transition. *Research in Post-compulsory Education* 16 (3): 385–396.

Löwith, K. 1993. *Marx and Weber*. London: Routledge.

Machin, S., and K. Salvanes. 2010. *Valuing school quality via school choice reform*. London: Centre for the Economics of Education.

Machin, S., and J. Vernoit. 2011. *Changing school autonomy: Academy schools and their introduction to England's education*. London: Centre For The Economics of Education.

Marklund, L. 2015. Preschool teachers' informal online professional development in relation to educational use of tablets in Swedish preschools. *Professional Development in Education* 41 (2): 236–253.

Mayo, P. 2013. *Echoes from Freire for a critically engaged pedagogy*. London: Bloomsbury.

McCrone, T., C. Southcott, and N. George. 2011. *Governance models in schools: Local government education and children's services*. Slough: NFER.

Olssen, M., J.A. Codd, and M.A. O'Neill. 2004. *Education policy: Globalisation, citizenship and democracy*. London: Sage.

Saunders, D.B. 2010. Neoliberal ideology and public education in the United States. *The Journal of Critical Education Policy Studies* 8 (1): 42–77.

Selwyn, N. 2011. The place of technology in the conservative-Liberal democrat education agenda: An ambition of absence? *Educational Review* 63 (4): 395–408.

Simmons, R. 2010. Globalisation, neo-liberalism and vocational learning: The case of further education colleges. *Research in Post-compulsory Education* 15 (4): 363–376.

Smith, A. 1991. *The wealth of nations*. London: Everyman.

Torres, C.A. 1998. *Democracy, education and multiculturalism*. Lanham: Rowman and Littlefield.

———. 2008. *Education and neoliberal globalisation*. New York: Taylor and Francis.

Urban, M. 2009. Strategies for change: rethinking professional development to meet the challenges of diversity in the early years profession. Paper presented at the IPDA conference, 27–28 November, Birmingham, UK.

Vermunt, J.D. 2016. Keynote address. Paper presented at the IPDA conference, 25–26 November, Stirling, UK.

CHAPTER 2

Neoliberalism and Early Years

INTRODUCTION

This chapter investigates the application of technology to pedagogy in early years (with children aged from birth to eight years of age). The chapter content considers the perceptions of technology that are held by a variety of practitioners in a range of settings and in different cultural contexts. The research in the chapter is drawn from key literature that has been published on the application of technology to pedagogy in early years and the associated tensions that exist between policy and practice (for example Bers 2008; Drotner et al. 2008; Goldberg et al. 2003; Kirkwood and Price 2014; Marsh et al. 2005; Plowman and Stephen 2005; Prensky 2001; Yelland and Kilderry 2010). The chapter explores the factors influencing the interpretation of the pedagogical value of technology by reflecting on two key questions that are asked in the work of Ingleby et al. (2019). Do the educators follow neoliberal policymakers who support the application of technology to pedagogy? Do the educators mirror academic research in this area by considering that 'e' is only 'best' when it is applied to pedagogy to develop creative thinking? The chapter draws on research about the experiences of educators who are working in a variety of early years settings in different cultural contexts. The chapter reveals that a complex range of personal, social and professional factors influence the educators' pedagogy with technology. It is argued that the

E. Ingleby, *Neoliberalism Across Education*, Palgrave Studies on Global Policy and Critical Futures in Education, https://doi.org/10.1007/978-3-030-73962-1_2

tensions that exist between the educators and the neoliberal policymakers are a consequence of the policymakers omitting to see the complex range of factors that appear to influence successful pedagogy with technology in the early years. With regards to one example of this complexity, Yelland and Kilderry (2010) reveal that much pedagogical thought needs to go into considering how children's thinking processes are being developed by technology. It is argued that if this philosophical reflection is not informing the pedagogy in this sector of education, then the subsequent application of technology to pedagogy is not necessarily achieving anything special in terms of the cognitive development of the learners. The process becomes akin to the tale of the emperor's new clothes where there is nothing other than an illusion of there being something special taking place. A key theme in the chapter is that there is an absence of pedagogical philosophy in the neoliberal policymakers' recommendation that applying technology to pedagogy in early years education is akin to best pedagogical practice. Within the chapter, it is argued that the processes of pedagogy that are required to apply technology to pedagogy successfully, so that children's cognitive abilities are developed effectively, are not considered fully by the neoliberal policymakers. It is argued that there are examples (for instance, in The English Conservative Party pre-election manifesto 2017) where it is assumed that 'e is best' without reflecting upon why 'e is best'. There appears to be the simple assumption that the application of technology to pedagogy is best practice simply because it is best practice. This misleading tautology demonstrates that the neoliberal policymakers are interpreting pedagogy with technology in incredibly simplistic ways and the unfortunate consequence that is revealed in the literature is an occurrence of tension between policy and practice that results in negativity.

In the chapter, it is argued that although technology is a major feature of contemporary neoliberal policy, the strategies that are necessary to apply technology successfully to pedagogy in the early years are not always clear and apparent. The chapter develops the argument that effective pedagogy with technology depends upon nurturing leadership, scholarship and professional identity. This then holds the potential to enable the sense of effective pedagogy that Marsh et al. (2005) and Yelland and Kilderry (2010) reflect on. As previously noted, the pre-election English Conservative Party Manifesto (2015) makes 17 references to technology and there are 30 references to technology in the 2017 manifesto alongside 15 references to technology in the 2019 pre-election manifesto. 'Technology' is regarded as being favourable in its own right and there is much emphasis placed on the importance of 'technical education' (2017, 52). The classical neoliberal themes are present within this manifesto document as technology becomes linked to 'industrial opportunity' (2017, 23) and technology is considered to be beneficial for 'teachers in the preparation of lessons and marking' (2017, 51, cited in Ingleby et al. 2019). The research in this chapter considers these neoliberal policy recommendations alongside reflecting on the complex range of personal, social, and professional factors that appear to inform early years practitioners and their pedagogy with technology. The chapter is informed by the work of seminal world-leading research texts that have developed research in this area (including the work of Kirkup and Kirkwood [2005]; Kirkwood and Price [2014]; Prensky [2001]). The chapter applies the work of these authors by arguing that the neoliberal policymakers' support for applying technology in pedagogy is not necessarily shared by the academic researchers or the early years practitioners and their students. It is argued that the factors that are influencing pedagogy with technology are incredibly complex and the chapter content reveals a series of challenges that are present for educators within the early years in view of the tension that appears in neoliberal policies and pedagogical practice.

TECHNOLOGY, PEDAGOGY, AND NEOLIBERALISM

If we are to understand neoliberal approaches to technology and pedagogy it is helpful to exemplify a neoliberal context that has a rich heritage of policies about technology and pedagogy. It is argued that the neoliberal policymakers in England have a particularly keen interest in developing the application of technology to pedagogy (Selwyn 2011). As noted, the current Conservative government in England have endorsed the application of technology in pedagogy. 'Security for families' is linked to 'jobs' that will be created via 'investing in science and technology' (Conservative Party Manifesto 2015, 17). Indeed, an explicit neoliberal policy aim is to 'make Britain the new technology centre of Europe' (Conservative Party Manifesto 2015, 21). There is a general view expressed by the policymakers in the English neoliberal context that technology enables 'everyone' to 'rise as high as their talents and effort can take them' (Conservative Party Manifesto 2015, 81). However, this current neoliberal endorsement of the importance of technology can be traced back over decades in England. It is a trend that has gathered momentum so that it is an important element in neoliberal approaches to educational policy in England. In exemplifying a neoliberal context that equates technology and pedagogy as desirable, this section of the chapter summarises the development and the subsequent rise in importance of pedagogy with technology in England.

In the English educational context, there has been neoliberal policy-maker support for applying technology to pedagogy for a number of years. Jones (1980) is one of a number of academics who reveals that the message that technology is good for pedagogy has been encouraged over time. From 1950 onwards there has been investment in educational technology by neoliberal governments in England and this appears to have laid the foundations for the significant investment in technology for pedagogy that occurred under the Conservative administrations from 1979 onwards. This resulted in microcomputers being introduced within schools in England. The reason for this pedagogical initiative is explained simply: 'so that our young people are skilled at an early age' (Thatcher 1983, cited in Ingleby 2015, 145). What is important about this statement is that there is no subsequent explanation for how these 'young people' are to become 'skilled at an early age'. This reveals a significant gap that exists between providing the technological resources without advising about the sort of pedagogical techniques that ought to be utilised if the technology is to be effective. To draw on an analogy, this appears to be similar to providing fertiliser without giving any explanation as to how the fertiliser can be used to enhance the growth and development of plants.

Nevertheless, despite an absence of pedagogical philosophy, it is argued by Selwyn (2011) that the Thatcher administrations were at least consistent in England in producing a series of policies that increased the use of technology within the education system in England. However, the thinking behind how the technology could be used to develop the skills of both the learners and their educators is not apparent and this reveals a key aspect of neoliberal approaches to educational policy in general, both in England and in other cultural contexts (for example, in the United States of America as revealed by Bers [2008] and in Australia as noted by Yelland and Kilderry [2010]). An intervention occurs, however, the recommendations that are necessary to develop and nurture the intervention are not present. A key theme of this chapter is that the cognitive needs of the learners and their teachers have not been taken into consideration following this particular neoliberal policy intervention. This argument is exemplified with the Thatcher administration's 1981 Micros in Schools scheme. This neoliberal educational policy resulted in in over 4000 schools ordering microcomputers by 1992, however, the provision of the technology was not supported by considering how to address the pedagogical developmental needs of the teachers. It is argued that the teachers' subsequent professional development needs were 'neglected' (Marsh et al. 2005, 69). The neoliberal policy of providing computers for schools because technology is inherently good in its own right is further evidenced through the establishment of the National Council for Educational Technology by the Conservative administration at the end of the 1980s. It is argued by Clegg et al. (2003) that in England, although pedagogy with computers has become accepted at political levels, more needs to be done in order to think through the purpose of introducing computers into schools. In other words, although there has been consistent support for using technology in pedagogy in England, more needs to be done if the pedagogy is to be successful in respect of developing the cognitive abilities of the children (Wild and King 1999).

In England, the New Labour administrations from 1997–2010 continued to champion the application of technology to pedagogy (Selwyn 2011) and the key themes of New Labour's approach to pedagogy with technology are apparent in David Blunkett's Greenwich Speech. Technology is referred to in positive ways in its links to globalisation and its seismic effects in enabling economic growth (Blunkett 2000). Under New Labour, the neoliberal interventions of the Blair and Brown administrations were characterised by intense educationally focused programmes that were based on applying technology to pedagogy (for example The Every Child Matters policy agenda and its educational curriculum development The Early Years Foundation Stage equate economic development with enhancing technology skills). However, once again, the gap that exists between providing technology and meeting the pedagogical needs of the practitioners and their students does not appear to have been closed.

Moreover, despite a shift in neoliberal policy aims to cutting public spending and efficiency savings, from 2010–2015 the English Coalition government still continued to reinforce the importance of the use of technology in education in similar ways to previous administrations. Despite the occurrence of what Selwyn refers to as a 'bonfire of the quangos' (Selwyn 2011 cited in Ingleby 2015, 146) the application of technology to pedagogy has still received neoliberal government support. Although political administrations have changed, a consistent message is apparent in England, that technology ought to be used in education, without considering the merits or otherwise of this educational policy approach.

TECHNOLOGY PEDAGOGY AND EARLY YEARS

The literature about pedagogy with technology reveals that a complex range of personal, social, and professional factors influence pedagogy with technology in the early years (some of the key literature that has been consulted includes Bers 2008; Drotner et al. 2008; Goldberg et al. 2003; Marsh et al. 2005; Plowman and Stephen 2005; Prensky 2001; Yelland and Kilderry 2010). The literature is characterised by the theme of the complexity that appears to be present in pedagogy with technology. Moreover, in the work of Harland and Kinder (2014) and Macfarlane and Cartmel (2012), it is revealed that the associated professional development needs of the educators are not being met by neoliberal policymakers. This appears to be part of the missing gap that was referred to in the previous sections of the chapter. In the work of Harland and Kinder (2014) and Macfarlane and Cartmel (2012) it is argued that effective professional development is dependent upon nurturing educational leadership, scholarship and professional identity and in this chapter it is argued that the simple provision of neoliberal policies about applying technology to pedagogy does little to nurture this area of pedagogy. The subsequent section of this chapter summarises the key themes in general that are associated with this literature on applying technology to pedagogy in early years in neoliberal contexts.

The published research on applying technology to pedagogy in early years education consistently draws attention to the importance of reflecting on the pedagogical processes that are being used with technology in helping to develop children's cognitive skills. Education in the early years has been informed by a number of pedagogical philosophies, including the ideas of Maria Montessori and the Reggio Emilia form of pedagogy. Both of these examples of pedagogy are based on tried and tested forms of teaching and learning, where particular pedagogical practices help in developing the physical, intellectual, emotional, and social development of children. Therefore, much of the literature on applying technology to pedagogy reflects on the processes of teaching and learning that are being generated by the application of technology to pedagogy. This theme of reflecting on the pedagogical processes that are being applied with technology is evident in the work of Bers (2008), and Yelland and Kilderry (2010). Bers (2008) offers a profound reflection on the application of technology to pedagogy in early years in her research compared to the simple recommendation 'that our young people are skilled at an early age'

(Thatcher 1983, cited in Ingleby 2015, 145). As opposed to recommending the provision of technology in teaching spaces, Bers (2008) argues that this technology can only become useful if the educators and the children are enabled to work together to produce a shared synergy of creative learning and teaching. In this research (Bers 2008), a form of 'so what?' is asked that is not evident in the neoliberal policy recommendations. As opposed to focusing on the provision of computers in teaching spaces, there is an emphasis placed upon considering how the technology is being used to develop the cognitive abilities of the learners. In the work of Bers (2008), pedagogical processes with technology are identified that hold the capacity to develop cognitive abilities. Bers (2008) reveals that if children are enabled to design virtual worlds with technology this does appear to help in developing their cognitive abilities, however, what is important is not the technology in itself: it is the pedagogical processes that are occurring that are important. In other words, in this particular example of pedagogy in the early years (the research of Bers 2008), there is a clear pedagogical philosophy that is informing the application of technology to pedagogy. Bers (2008) develops the work of Goldberg et al. (2003) who argue for the importance of ensuring that technology is used in order to complement the wider pedagogical processes that are happening and that this synthesis of learning is helpful in developing the thinking processes of children. If this emphasis is placed on the processes of pedagogy there can be the occurrence of what Yelland Kilderry (2010) refer to as multidimensional and creative children's learning. The literature on the processes of pedagogy with technology is also informed by the work of Drotner et al. (2008) via their exploration of the perceptions of technology that are held by practitioners. Drotner et al. (2008) reveal that in contrast to the simple neoliberal policymaker recommendation of the importance of applying technology to pedagogy, a whole range of personal and professional factors appear to influence how this dominant neoliberal policymaker discourse is received by the educators. In other words, a rich tapestry that is informed by a complex range of factors appears to inform the application of technology to pedagogy. Moreover, the work of Marsh et al. (2005, 76) reveals that 'gender' is another complex facet influencing the application of technology to pedagogy. Marsh et al. (2005) argue that traditionally, technology has been associated with males and not females and that this socio-cultural aspect of applying technology to pedagogy ought to be taken into consideration. In this respect (the focus on socio-cultural factors), the work of Marsh et al. (2005) complements Prensky's (2001) argument that there may be digital natives (who are familiar with technology) and digital immigrants (who are less familiar with technology) and that all of these complex sociocultural factors ought to be taken into account if we are to nurture pedagogy with technology in the early years. Earlier in the chapter, reference was made to equating neoliberal recommendations to apply technology to pedagogy as being akin to the tale of the emperor's new clothes and this analogy is also made by Clegg et al. (2003).

Alongside the complex range of socio-cultural factors that appear to influence the application of technology to pedagogy, Macfarlane and Cartmel (2012) draw attention to the absence of policies that nurture professional development in this area of education. Macfarlane and Cartmel (2012) argue that there are forms of professional development in education that have the capacity to be transformative of professional practice and in their research they outline the 'circles of change' and 'circles of change revisited' professional development initiatives (Macfarlane and Cartmel 2012, 845). Essentially, the 'circles of change' professional development initiative that enables a thinking space to consider the socio-cultural factors influencing professional practice in the University sector is applied by Macfarlane and Cartmel (2012) to early years practitioners in a new cultural context in Australia. The COC (or Circles of Change) model of professional development provides a thinking space for academics, students and professionals to reflect together on how the workplace can become an environment that encourages what is referred to as 'reciprocal and informative learning' (Macfarlane and Cartmel 2012, 846). Essentially the COC initiative is based on 'deconstructing' theory related to practice alongside confronting personal, social and systemic' issues that are associated with 'untouchable topics' (Macfarlane and Cartmel 2012, 847). Professional development is visualised as being a means of enabling the practitioners to think differently about their about their professional practice. It is argued that this innovative way of thinking about professional practice facilitates the educators to consider the complex range of factors influencing professional practice that are frequently absent within neoliberal policymaker recommendations. The work of Macfarlane and Cartmel (2012) complements the research of Harland and Kinder (2014, 672) and their reflection on the profound 'affective outcomes' that influence professional practice. These 'affective outcomes' are associated with the emotional factors that are involved with professional practice that hold the potential to produce what are referred to as 'zones of uncertainty' (Harland

and Kinder 2014, 673). The research of Macfarlane and Cartmel (2012) and Harland and Kinder (2014) once more reveals that more is needed than simply providing technology for educators and students in early years if this neoliberal policy is to become useful. Alongside considering how the technology is to be used, it is also necessary to reflect on how we can enable as positive an involvement with the curriculum as possible if pedagogy with technology is to become effective.

In the next section of the chapter, the key themes from the research that is associated with pedagogy and technology and early years education in neoliberal contexts is amplified following this initial summary. The challenge appears to rest within making the pedagogy creative so that children's cognitive abilities are developed (Bers 2008; Goldberg et al. 2003; Yelland and Kilderry 2010). In order to achieve this aim, it is essential to consider the interpretations of technology that are shared by the educators (as is evident in the work of Marsh et al. 2005; Kirkup and Kirkwood 2005; Kirkwood and Price 2014; Prensky 2001; Plowman and Stephen 2005). Moreover, the importance of generating a thinking space to reflect on professional practice is recommended by Harland and Kinder (2014) and Macfarlane and Cartmel (2012). The research from the authors who have been cited draws attention to the complex range of factors influencing pedagogy with technology in the early years and this contrasts with the neoliberal policymakers' simplistic tautology that 'e-learning is best' because 'it is best'.

Key Research Findings on Applying Technology to Pedagogy in the Early Years

The research that has been consulted on applying technology to pedagogy reveals three significant themes and this section of the chapter amplifies these themes in order to develop the argument that when neoliberal policymakers wish to intervene directly in educational policies the intervention ought to be based on pedagogical principles. To act upon the view that technology is good for pedagogy without having a sound basis for this action can result in problems in education, because the policy intervention is not based on sound research evidence. In this chapter, it is argued that the tensions that occur between the neoliberal policymakers and the educators are in general a consequence of an intervention that has been made by policymakers who are not educators. It appears that the recommendations to apply technology to pedagogy are not being supported by educational research and the three themes that are amplified in this section of the chapter are as follows:

1. Technology must be used in creative and innovative ways with a sound pedagogical philosophy that develops pedagogical processes if its application is to be successful.
2. The complex personal and socio-cultural factors influencing the application of technology to pedagogy need to be acknowledged if we are to develop a sound pedagogical philosophy in this area.
3. Alongside making interventions in pedagogy, neoliberal policymakers ought to provide recommendations for how professional development can be enabled, supported and nurtured.

1. Using technology creatively.

The success that rests behind any form of pedagogy appears to come from the presence of a sound philosophy of pedagogy that has been developed through processes of trial and error and is in turn used to advance future successful pedagogical processes. There are examples of these forms of pedagogy that are noted earlier in the Montessori and Reggio Emilia approaches to pedagogy. A number of European countries appear to base their pedagogy on processes that appear to work, for example as is evident in the Scandinavian pedagogy that is applied to the early years in Steiner settings and develops 'a space that is conducive to child-initiated activities' (Parker-Rees et al. 2010, 83). In the work of Bers (2008); Goldberg et al. (2003); Yelland and Kilderry (2010); it is revealed that this form of pedagogy has not necessarily occurred in the United States, the United Kingdom or Australia. It appears that the neoliberal policymakers produce what Brown et al. (2015) critique as being a less than helpful manifestation of power in education in the early years. Whereas the Reggio Emilia learning environment evidences pedagogical processes that are based on practice and repetition in order to meet the cognitive needs of the children, pedagogy with technology in the early years in neoliberal contexts is not always based on creative forms of teaching and learning. In the research of Bers (2008) it is revealed that technology can be used to develop the cognitive abilities of the children, however, thought needs to be given to the sort of learning activities that are occurring and the subsequent forms of thinking processes that are being developed. Bers (2008) outlines that this can occur if the children are enabled to construct virtual worlds using what is referred to as second-life technology. However, these pedagogical activities are frequently occurring in stand-alone ways and Goldberg et al. (2003) reveal that technology is not always used in ways that support the wider curriculum processes. A disconnect appears to occur between the application of technology in pedagogy and the wider curriculum objectives. In contrast whereas teaching philosophies in the early years like Montessori, Reggio Emilia, and Steiner appear to be based on a whole sense of the curriculum (Parker-Rees et al. 2010), the learning activities with technology in the early years tend to be associated with interventions that are not supported with a whole sense that the wider curriculum is being developed. This is revealed by Yelland and Kilderry (2010) when they exemplify activities with technology that are used in the curriculum, however their application is based on a unidimensional approach to learning that does not make multidimensional connections with the rest of the curriculum. This develops the argument that it is essential to have a whole view of how technology can be used to develop the wider curriculum as opposed to having a focus that is in any way narrow or restricted. Like all resources, technology can develop cognitive skills, however thought is necessary for what is being developed and how the development is occurring.

2. Personal and socio-cultural factors influencing pedagogy with technology.

It is also evident in the research that has been completed on applying technology to pedagogy that a whole complex range of personal, and socio-cultural factors influence how the technology is used and what can be achieved via technological pedagogy. In contrast to the mere provision of technology for pedagogy, it is important to reflect on how these complex personal and socio-cultural factors are influencing what is happening within the learning spaces. It may be possible to provide second-life technology to every child who is being taught within an early years setting, however the impact of the provision of this technology will be influenced by the personal, socio-cultural characteristics of the learners and their educators. Each of the educators will have particular impressions of what can be achieved via applying technology to pedagogy and this argument is made by Drotner et al. (2008). Moreover, the practitioners who are working in the early years may have complex and conflicting interpretations of what is technology and how this technology can be applied to pedagogy in this area (Plowman and Stephen 2005). The varying interpretations of technology and whether or not the labels 'Information Technoloy', or 'Information Communication Technology' should be used will differ across groups of educators. The work of Plowman and Stephen (2005) is complemented by Kirkup and Kirkwood (2005) and Kirkwood and Price (2014) in their argument that the best way of considering what is happening when technology is applied to learning spaces is to refer to this practice as a form of 'TEL' or 'Technology Enabled Learning'. Alongside the practical challenges of defining what technology enabled learning is, wider socio-cultural factors (for example gender) appear to influence pedagogy with technology. Authors including McKie et al. (2001) draw attention to the importance of gender in shaping perceptions of what is happening during social interactions and the work of Marsh et al. (2005) reveals that gender is a significant factor in the interpretation of pedagogy with technology. Marsh et al. (2005) argue that traditionally, technology is associated with the male world and that this perception can influence views on who should use technology and how successful technological interventions are likely to be. This work on social factors and technology with pedagogy is also associated with the work of Prensky (2001) and the argument that there are digital natives and digital immigrants. Although, today in England, we might argue that most people have become fluent with technology, there are nevertheless those who are unfamiliar and/or resistant to technology. The work of Prensky (2001) reveals the complex personal and socio-cultural variables that influence the application of technology to pedagogy. Without taking these factors into consideration, the subsequent pedagogy with technology that occurs cannot be fully developed or enhanced. It is necessary to do more than simply make technology available in early years settings. Alongside considering how technology can be used to develop children's thinking processes, it is also necessary to consider the complex personal, and socio-cultural factors that are influencing the application of technology to pedagogy.

3. Professional development and pedagogy with technology.

It is also essential to ensure that thought is provided as to how professional development with technology and pedagogy can be developed. This appears to be an area that has not been thought about fully and there is a gap between the research on pedagogy with technology, how this research can be used to develop teaching with technology, and moreover, how the CPD needs of the educators can be enhanced in the future through effective professional development. The research in this area (for example Carmichael and Procter 2006; Harland and Kinder 2014; Leask and Younie 2013; Macfarlane and Cartmel 2012; Procter 2007) draws attention to the absence of transformative professional development in this area. If there is to be coherent professional development with technology and pedagogy, it is important to ensure that the neoliberal policymaker interventions are based on credible research and that this research is being used to subsequently develop teaching with technology. However, it appears to be the case that the policymaker interventions occur without due consideration for pedagogy or professional development. The tension and negativity that can appear in early years professional practice in England appears to be an unfortunate consequence of the gaps that exist between policy, pedagogy and professional development. The research in this chapter (for example the work of Drotner et al. 2008) draws attention to the socio-cultural factors influencing pedagogy with technology, however these affective factors do not appear to be have been subsumed within a comprehensive approach to the professional development of educators in the early years. The thinking space that can be created by the COC initiative Macfarlane and Cartmel (2012) reflect on is captured within one isolated research study and there does not appear to be a comprehensive approach to developing professional practice in education by the neoliberal policymakers in England. Vermunt (2016) exemplifies an example of the type of transformative professional development that ought to occur in this area with his reflection on the impact of the Japanese lesson plan. In this particular form of professional development, the teachers and the students come together to plan teaching sessions and to observe what happens in practice from this initial planning activity. The subsequent pedagogy is nurtured and developed as a result of reflecting on what changes through the reflections of the teachers and the students. This example of transformative professional development is necessary if the research that has been completed on pedagogy with technology is to be developed in the future. This then becomes a way of uniting disparate occurrences in a neoliberal context, where the research is not always informing professional practice and its subsequent processes of professional development.

CONCLUDING DISCUSSION

If we apply the work of Goffman (1971) to help in understanding what is happening with neoliberalism and early years education, we can regard pedagogy with technology as being akin to types of performance. There are examples of what Goffman (1971, 26) refers to as 'dramaturgical problems', the defining problem being the application of technology in order to realise effective pedagogy. Although some elements of pedagogy are pre-scripted (for example the interaction that unfolds during the processes of pedagogy) other important elements of the pedagogy are a consequence of the neoliberal policymakers and their interventions. The educators and the students are generating learning *in situ and* improvising during pedagogical activities. Mistakes can be made by policymakers, educators and learners so there is never a sense of 'infallibility' (Goffman 1971, 52) in respect of pedagogy with technology and the professional development supporting this form of pedagogy. The pedagogy that occurs with technology in neoliberal contexts can be viewed as being rationally grasped activities that are generated by policymakers, educators, and learners as opposed to being visualised as a passive 'mode of participation' (Dewey 2004, 323).

Leask and Younie (2013, 274 cited in Ingleby 2015, 152) emphasise the importance of generating a 'research-informed knowledge base' to inform the subsequent development of pedagogy and the authors who are cited in this chapter (for example Bers 2008; Drotner et al. 2008; Goldberg et al. 2003; Kirkwood and Price 2014; Marsh et al. 2005; Plowman and Stephen 2005; Prensky 2001; Yelland and Kilderry 2010) have done this. It is now important to develop pedagogy with technology in early years in neoliberal contexts by using this research and this is recommended in order to develop teaching and learning (Leask and Younie). One suggestion that is made by Leask and Younie (2013) is to establish an e-infrastructure that is shaped by practitioners and policymakers so that pedagogy with technology can be developed. In other words, as opposed to saying that pedagogy with technology is inherently good, reflections can be made on what is being achieved by pedagogy with technology and why this achievement is occurring.

This chapter has made reference to the work of Harland and Kinder (2014, 672) and the importance of the 'affective outcomes' (those personal and social factors influencing professional work) that influence pedagogy and the subsequent professional development of the educators. It is important to take into consideration these 'affective outcomes' that are influencing pedagogy with technology in early years in order to ensure that 'zones of uncertainty' in pedagogy with technology are considered as fully as possible (Harland and Kinder 2014, 673). The published research on pedagogy with technology reveals that there are social circumstances influencing the application of technology to pedagogy (for example, Plowman and Stephen 2005). These social factors influence interaction in education and elsewhere (McKie et al. 2001) and they contribute to the educators and the learners reflecting on the application of technology to pedagogy as opposed to simply assuming that e is best. The research on pedagogy with technology reveals that the educators and the learners do not simply do what they are told to do by the neoliberal policymakers (Ingleby 2015). A more complex set of dramaturgical challenges appear to be influencing pedagogy with technology in early years in neoliberal contexts.

Leask and Younie (2013, 280) recommend introducing an 'online environment' in order to promote shared teaching resources for pedagogy with technology. The purpose of this 'resource' is to enable educators to 'move between different communities in the same environment' (Leask and Younie 2013, 280). This technology resource is envisaged as allowing educators to network and reflect on developing pedagogy with technology. It is argued by Leask and Younie (2013) that this subsequent reflection will foster a sharing of ideas between educators, researchers and policymakers about pedagogy with technology. This recommendation is also supported by Carmichael and Procter (2006) and Procter (2007). The thinking behind this recommendation is based on a wish to have those who are educating shaping the policies about pedagogy. The research on pedagogy with technology that is cited in this chapter draws attention to the importance of ensuring that we reflect on the complex range of factors influencing pedagogy with technology so that we can in turn develop pedagogical practice in this area. It is argued by Ingleby (2015) that it is too simplistic to assume that the mere provision of online resources will develop pedagogy with technology. The research of Ingleby et al. (2019) reveals that the nature of the educational setting (its philosophy and its habitus) contributes to the effectiveness (or otherwise) of the pedagogy that is occurring. Moreover, the characteristics of the educators and the learners come together to shape pedagogy in this area and yet the neoliberal policymakers do not appear to grasp fully how these characteristics are shaping pedagogy with technology. No matter how innovative the online resources for professional development may be, their application appears to be linked to the support that the educators receive within the setting. The 15 references to technology that appear in The Conservative Party Manifesto in 2019 refer to 'investing in technology' (2019, 2), however there is no explanation given as to how this investment in technology will be beneficial for educators and their students. The 'wish' for 'investment in education, infrastructure and technology, to create a high-age, high-skill, low-tax economy' (2019, 3), alongside the proposed establishment of '20 Institutes of Technology' (2019, 36) does not appear to be informed by a philosophy of pedagogy and its subsequent professional development. To draw on the work of Goffman (1971), it is as if the actors in the play do not know the lines that are required for the successful performance of the play.

The chapter began by exemplifying a neoliberal context (England) which has consistently witnessed the intervention by neoliberal policy-makers in education so that technology is introduced into educational settings. There has been a consistent support for pedagogy with technology in England from 1979 until 2019 over a period of 40 years. In the 2019 Conservative Party manifesto reference is made to the UK being 'Europe's technology capital, producing start-ups and success stories at a dazzling pace' (2019, 28). However, in contrast to this acceptance of the importance of technology for pedagogy, the published research literature in this area questions the need for applying technology to pedagogy. The overwhelming consensus appears to be that technology is only useful for pedagogy when there is a coherent philosophy behind its application (Bers 2008; Drotner et al. 2008; Goldberg et al. 2003; Marsh et al. 2005; Yelland and Kilderry 2010). The published research on this area draws attention to the many complex variables that appear to influence the success or otherwise of pedagogy with technology. The work of Mercer et al. (2019) reveals that digital technology holds the potential for supporting dialogic pedagogy where language is used for reasoning and learning, however, the technology has to be used with this purpose in mind. It is the pedagogy that is crucial to the successful implementation of technology for learning as opposed to the technology in itself. Mercer et al. (2019) argue that technology ought to be used with the purpose of enabling pedagogical activities that are designed well so that they promote collective thinking. The content of this chapter reveals that these complex personal, social and professional factors need to be taken into consideration if pedagogy with technology is to be effective. Whether or not this occurs in neoliberal contexts in early years appears to depend on whether or not a coherent philosophy of pedagogy is informing the application of technology to pedagogy and its subsequent professional development.

REFERENCES

Bers, M. 2008. *Blocks to robots: Learning with technology in the early childhood classroom.* New York: Teachers College Press.

Blunkett, D. 2000. Greenwich speech. Department for Education and Employment. Accessed July 20, 2019. http://www.cms1.gre.ac.uk/dfee/#speech.

Brown, C., Y. Lan, and H. In Jeong. 2015. Beginning to entangle the strange coupling of power within a neoliberal early education context. *International Journal of Early Years Education* 23 (2): 138–152.

Carmichael, P., and R. Procter. 2006. IT for education research: Using new technology to enhance a complex research programme. London: Institute of Education. Accessed July 20, 2019. http://www.tlrp.org/pub/documents/no16_procter.pdf.

Clegg, S., A. Hudson, and J. Steel. 2003. The emperor's new clothes: Globalisation and e-learning in higher education. *British Journal of Sociology of Education* 24 (1): 39–53.

Conservative Party Manifesto. 2015. Strong leadership, a clear economic plan, a brighter more secure future. Accessed June 1, 2015. https://www.conservatives.com/Manifesto.

———. 2017. Forward together: our plan for a stronger Britain and a more prosperous future. Accessed October 9, 2017. https://www.conservatives.com/Manifesto.

———. 2019. Get brexit done unleash Britain's potential. Accessed November 25, 2019. https://feweek.co.uk/wp-content/uploads/2019/11/Conservative2019Manifesto.pdf.

Dewey, J. 2004. *Democracy and education.* Mineola, N.Y: Dover.

Drotner, K., H. Siggaard Jensen, and K. Christian Schroder. 2008. *Informal learning and digital media.* Newcastle: Cambridge Scholars Publishing.

Goffman, E. 1971. *The presentation of the self in everyday life.* London: Pelican Books.

Goldberg, A., M. Russell, and A. Cook. 2003. The effects of computers on students' writing: A meta-analysis from 1992–2002. *Journal of Technology Learning and Assessment* 2 (1): 1–52.

Harland, J., and K. Kinder. 2014. Teachers' continuing professional development: Framing a model of outcomes. *Professional Development in Education* 40 (4): 669–682.

Ingleby, E. 2015. The impact of changing policies about technology on the professional development needs of early years educators in England. *Professional Development in Education* 41 (1): 144–158.

Ingleby, E., B. Wilford, and C. Hedges. 2019. Teaching with technology and higher education: A brave new world? *Practice: Contemporary Issues in Practitioner Education* 1 (1): 73–87.

Jones, R. 1980. Microcomputers: Their uses in primary schools. *Cambridge Journal of Education* 10 (3): 144–153.

Kirkup, G., and A. Kirkwood. 2005. Information and communications technologies (ICT) in higher education teaching- a tale of gradualism rather than revolution. *Learning, Media and Technology* 30 (2): 185–199.

Kirkwood, A., and L. Price. 2014. Technology enhanced learning and teaching in higher education: What is 'enhanced' and how do we know? A critical literature review. *Learning, Media and Technology* 39 (1): 6–36.

Leask, M., and S. Younie. 2013. National models for continuing professional development: The challenges of twenty first century knowledge management. *Professional Development in Education* 39 (2): 273–287.

Macfarlane, K., and J. Cartmel. 2012. Circles of change revisited: Building leadership, scholarship and professional identity in the children's services sector. *Professional Development in Education* 38 (5): 845–861.

Marsh, J., G. Brooks, J. Hughes, L. Ritchie, S. Roberts, and K. Wright. 2005. *Digital beginnings: young children's use of popular culture, media and new technologies.* Sheffield: University of Sheffield Literacy Research Centre.

McKie, L., S. Bowlby, and S. Gregory. 2001. Gender, caring and employment in Britain. *Journal of Social Policy* 30 (2): 233–258.

Mercer, N., S. Hennessy, and P. Warwick. 2019. Dialogue, thinking together and digital technology in the classroom: Some educational implications of a continuing line of inquiry. *International Journal of Educational Research* 97: 187–199.

Parker-Rees, R., C. Leeson, J. Willan, and J. Savage. 2010. *Early childhood studies.* 3rd ed. Exeter: Learning Matters.

Plowman, L., and C. Stephen. 2005. Children, play and computers in pre-school education. *British Journal of Educational Technology* 36 (2): 145–157.

Prensky, M. 2001. Digital natives. Digital immigrants part 1. *On the Horizon* 9 (5): 1–6.

Procter, R. 2007. Collaboration, coherence and capacity-building: The role of DSpace in supporting and understanding the TLRP. *Technology, Pedagogy and Education* 16 (3): 269–288.

Selwyn, N. 2011. The place of technology in the conservative-Liberal democrat education agenda: An ambition of absence? *Educational Review* 63 (4): 395–408.

Thatcher, M. 1983. Cited in Hansard House of Commons Parliamentary Questions—March 29, 1983 [40/177–82]. London: Hansard House of Commons.

Vermunt, J.D. 2016. Keynote address. Paper presented at the IPDA conference, 25–26 November, Stirling, UK.

Wild, P., and P. King. 1999. Education and IT policy: Virtual policy? In *Education policy and contemporary policy*, ed. J. Demaine, 175–195. Basingstoke: Macmillan Press.

Yelland, N., and A. Kilderry. 2010. Becoming numerate with information technologies in the twenty-first century. *International Journal of Early Years Education* 18 (2): 91–106.

CHAPTER 3

Neoliberalism and School Education

INTRODUCTION

This chapter also links to the research that was presented by Vermunt (2016) at the IPDA (International Professional Development Association) conference via the recommendation that we ought to listen to conversations in learning spaces about schools and their organisational culture if we are to enable the successful development of school education. It is argued that there are examples within neoliberalism where this listening to conversations about learning spaces is not evident. Within the chapter the theoretical work of Bernstein (2000) is considered to be a means of advancing knowledge as to why schools in England under neoliberal governments have chosen to prioritise the importance of academic results over a full sense of creative education. The chapter presents key elements of primary and secondary schools' organisational culture within the neoliberal context of England. The content considers the consequences of neoliberalism for the pedagogy that is occurring in primary and secondary schools in England. Within the chapter, it is argued that although there is the presence of a clear wish to obtain excellent educational standards in schools in England, there is also an absence of guidance from the neoliberal policymakers as to how this objective can be realised. A Hippocratic understanding of education is revealed by the neoliberal policymakers in England as it is considered that 'educational problems' can be 'cured'. In

E. Ingleby, *Neoliberalism Across Education*, Palgrave Studies on Global Policy and Critical Futures in Education, https://doi.org/10.1007/978-3-030-73962-1_3

the chapter it is argued that in measuring performance and results, the true complexity of educational processes in schools is misinterpreted. As opposed to being perceived as sages on stages, it is argued that school teachers in England need to be regarded as being akin to guides on the side if they are to meet the needs of their learners. However, this humanist model of pedagogy appears to be disregarded by the neoliberal policymakers in their wish to measure results. This in turn results in tension between the teachers and their students in the schools in England and the neoliberal policymakers.

The chapter is framed by a background of the financial pressures that have faced schools in England since the global financial crisis of 2007–2008. In England it is argued by the DfE (Department for Education) that good financial health in schools is vital for effective business management if we are to achieve successful outcomes for pupils. It was estimated by the DfE in 2016, that schools needed to save £1.3 billion in procurement, and £1.7 billion in workforce spending by 2019–2020. This equates to an 8% reduction in per-pupil funding for mainstream schools between 2019–2020 (National Audit Office 2017). The chapter is based on exploring the consequences that this neoliberal economic background has for schools in England in respect of the emphases that are considered to be important by the neoliberal policymakers. Education appears to be considered to be important in respect of helping to produce future workers for the economy. Bernstein (2000) draws attention to the importance of scientific education within the curriculum in neoliberal contexts. It is argued by Bernstein (2000) that this emphasis on the importance of objectivity in education in England is representative of a change that has occurred over time. Bernstein (2000) argues that the arts were traditionally considered to be more important than the scientific disciplines, however in England today it appears to be the case that those academic subjects that are interpreted as being particularly relevant for developing the skills of employability (for example mathematics and scientific disciplines) are regarded as being especially valuable and this has consequences for the academic curriculum. The result of this neoliberal emphasis on the importance of scientific education and the relegation of the arts to being interpreted as being of less importance is also explored within the work of Randall and Downie (1996). It is argued that this neoliberal interpretation of the world is based on what are referred to as Hippocratic understandings within health, care, and education. There is, in other words a primacy attached to scientific interpretations of the world. Randall and Downie (1996) argue that in neoliberal contexts like England, the ideals of Hippocrates are favoured over those of Asclepius who is associated with 'healing'. Healing is subjective and non-scientific whereas Hippocratic ways of solving problems are reliant upon science and reason. In schools in England, this is translated into an emphasis being placed upon what can be measured, so that results and performance and end-products become all important objectives. Coffield (2006b) and Guilford (1967) reflect on the implications of this scientific emphasis for the curriculum. There appears to be less importance being placed on education that is enterprising, or in other words, a curriculum that encourages students to think about the curriculum in ways that are creative and innovative. This, once again links to the work of Vermunt (2016) and the emphasis that is placed upon the importance of listening as opposed to simply accepting that scientific subjects are the best because they are interpreted as equipping the students with the skills that are necessary if they are to become effective workers for the future good of the economy. Although the chapter focuses on England, the content is relevant for a broader international audience as there are related themes that link to other neoliberal cultural contexts (for example, as noted in Chap. 1, this specific work is relevant to the broader research findings of Colmer et al. [2015] in Australia; Ilham et al. [2015] in the United States of America; and Marklund [2015] in Sweden). Therefore, this makes the chapter content relevant to neoliberal contexts beyond England.

Schools and Neoliberalism

As acknowledged previously in Chap. 1, this book is being written during a time when the primary and secondary schools in England are experiencing tremendous financial pressures. The research that was previously cited by the ATL (2017) in Chap. 1 reveals some of the funding pressures that are affecting primary and secondary schools in England, and it can be argued that these pressures are a direct consequence of neoliberal policymakers. The ATL (2017) and the NUT (2017) reveal that in the educational context of England, austerity is a neoliberal choice. In citing the global financial crisis of 2007–2008 and subsequently blaming the New Labour administrations that governed England from 1997–2010 for contributing to this global crisis, the Coalition and Conservative administrations that have held power in England since 2010 have been characterised by policies that have aimed at curtailing public spending. The ATL (2017) reveal that this has resulted in schools in England cutting their budgets.

Moreover, there are examples of schools in England that have had to dismiss teachers who are on temporary employment contracts because of this shortfall in funding (National Audit Office 2017). This lack of resourcing for schools appears to be a choice that has been made by neoliberal policymakers (Ingleby 2015a; Selwyn 2011). The ambition of absence that Selwyn (2011) discusses appears to be based on a philosophy that encourages the wider society beyond the state to complement the work that is occurring within the statutory sector. In the neoliberal context of England there has been an active policy encouragement to work in partnership with other sectors of the mixed economy of care so that the schools are governed in ways that are flexible and involve as wide a group of professionals as possible (McCrone et al. 2011). However, it can be argued that this governance model in schools is actually producing new class inequalities (Ball 2010), and that the impact this is having for the school ethos is in general highly negative (ATL 2017).

In deflecting attention away from the state, there appears to have been a rise in the accountability of teachers in primary and secondary schools in England (Glatter 2012). It is argued that measuring performance and results within the schools has turned into a preoccupation (Glatter 2012). In England there are league tables of schools that are judged to be outstanding; good; satisfactory; or unsatisfactory because of their educational performance and this has become a key theme within the English neoliberal educational context. Moreover, Glatter (2012) argues that this aspect of educational policy has continued to rise in importance over the years in England. However, despite the rise of the accountability of the primary and secondary schools in England, many of their organisational characteristics were unchanged for decades and this is exemplified with leadership structures (Gunter 2011). In consequence this has led to neoliberal policymakers implementing new models of governance for primary and secondary schools in England (Machin and Salvanes 2010). It is argued by Machin and Salvanes (2010) that neoliberal governments in England have attempted to enable choice in schools by withdrawing from the regulation of all aspects of the curriculum and that this attempt at enabling freedom from regulation is regarded as being a means whereby school quality can be enhanced (Machin and Salvanes 2010).

This neoliberal wish to change schools' organisational structures and to enable an ambition of absence is evident in the introduction of the academy school system that has occurred under neoliberal governments in England since 2002 (Machin and Vernoit 2011). These schools are free from regulation by central government in respect of having responsibility for managing their own budgets and making their own curriculum choices through being 'outside the control of local authorities' (Machin and Vernoit 2011, 2). Moreover, there are opportunities for groups of schools to come together to collaborate as academy chains and this evidences a philosophy of doing things differently that can be regarded as being innovative in certain respects. However, Machin and Vernoit (2011) refer to this neoliberal educational initiative as being controversial. The controversy appears to emanate from the governance system of the academy schools as the schools are sponsored beyond the local authorities. The work of Clarke (2014) raises questions about the potential nature of the sponsors of the academy schools in respect of who the sponsors are; what sort of curriculum is being introduced; and what is trying to be achieved? The work of Clarke (2014) in particular reveals the potential that the flexible arrangement of the academy schools has for the development of religious extremism. This appears to be a classic example of a neoliberal educational policy that is not based on a sound and coherent philosophy of pedagogy. In the previous chapter, reference was made to the educational philosophies that characterise the Montessori; Reggio Emilia; and Steiner approaches to education. These approaches to pedagogy appear to be grounded in clear conceptualisations about what works when we are educating children and conversely what ought to be avoided in the classroom. All three of these philosophies of education appear to focus on processes of pedagogy as opposed to concentrating on end products (Urban 2009). As previously noted, the ways of teaching the students are considered within the Montessori; Reggio Emilia; and Steiner approaches to pedagogy and these philosophies of pedagogy appear to have emerged from reflecting on successful ways of educating the students. In contrast, the academy school system of education that has been introduced into England by neoliberal policymakers since 2002 is an initiative that has been borrowed from the United States (Machin and Vernoit 2011). The academy schools appear to have been established because of concerns about the costs of public sector education, and the freedom that is encouraged in these schools connects to neoliberal political and economic agendas as opposed to being based on a philosophy of pedagogy. Urban (2009) reflects on such educational initiatives by making reference to the film 'The Wizard of Oz'. As opposed to considering processes in entirety, the neoliberal policymakers appear to focus on final destinations (in other words, by emphasising the importance of results and achievement or end products). In consequence there appears to be a void that is being filled with initiatives that are based on political and socio-economic imperatives. This section of the chapter reveals a number of key neoliberal policy characteristics that apply to primary and secondary education in schools in England and the subsequent section of the chapter considers some of the theoretical interpretations that are associated with neoliberalism and schools.

THEORETICAL INTERPRETATIONS OF NEOLIBERALISM AND SCHOOLS

The theoretical content of the chapter draws on Bernstein (2000) who accounts for why there is an emphasis being placed on the importance of achieving measurable results in primary and secondary schools in England. Aspects of the schools' organisational culture that are regarded as being peripheral to the priority goal of achieving successful academic results are considered to be less important, and Bernstein's (2000) work provides an explanation for why this is the case.

Bernstein (2000) argues that many of the challenges within education in England stem from what he refers to as a dislocation that exists between the Trivium and the Quadrivium. Bernstein (2000) reflects on the tension that is present in education in the West by arguing that the academic curriculum is a combination of Christian and Greek influences, and that these cultural traditions are characterised by contradiction. The Trivium (rhetoric, grammar, logic) can appear to be at odds with the Quadrivium (arithmetic, astronomy, geometry and music). Bernstein (2000) argues that what is subjective and impressionistic is associated with the Trivium and that the objective scientific world can be seen as a representation of the Quadrivium. In exemplifying this contradiction and tension, Bernstein (2000) reflects on the nature of the traditional University academic parades in England. It was those staff who were associated with the Quadrivium who led the academic parades, with the academic staff teaching the Trivium subjects following on behind. Bernstein (2000) argues that this ceremonial occurrence was designed to reinforce the importance of the Christological saying that the last shall be first and the first shall be last. Bernstein (2000) argues that Christianity is an unusual religion due to the belief that God became human. In England, divine mortality and flesh and blood became associated with the subjective and impressionistic subjects of the Trivium (Bernstein 2000). In consequence, in the traditional curriculum in England, the science based subjects of the Quadrivium were viewed as being of less (divine) importance. However, Bernstein (2000) reflects on the reversal in importance of the Trivium and Quadrivium in English education today. What is subjective and impressionistic and traditionally associated with the Trivium is now replaced by an emphasis being placed on what is measurable and quantifiable (Bernstein 2000).

It is worth acknowledging too that Bernstein's (2000) work is applied to the higher education sector by McLean et al. (2013) in order to understand the nature of higher educational contexts in neoliberal nation states. In this chapter, there is a development of the work of McLean et al. (2013) through the application of Bernsteinian concepts to schools' organisational culture in England and the subsequent reflection on the consequences for primary and secondary school education. In exemplifying this argument, the direct influence of neoliberal governments in England on education reveals that teaching in primary and secondary schools is not just about what Bernstein refers to as 'transmitting disciplinary knowledge' (McLean et al. 2013, 32). Teaching and learning are complex processes that are framed by social inclusion and political participation (Bernstein 2000). Within a curriculum teaching and learning occurs via what McLean et al. (2013, 33) refer to as 'accessing the knowledge and procedures of disciplines'. Bernstein's (2000) work is relevant for the chapter because it explores how the 'unequal distribution of knowledge in formal education systems relays inequalities in society' (McLean et al. 2013, 34). In applying Bernstein's (2000) work to the chapter, education in England can be regarded as being influenced by dispositions, values and outlooks and that this in turn affects 'thinking, feeling and action' (McLean et al. 2013, 34). In the previous section of the chapter and in Chap. 1, reference is made to the recent English neoliberal governments' 'ambition of absence' (Selwyn 2011, 365, cited in Ingleby 2015a). This chapter considers Bernstein's (2000) work by reflecting on 'how biases shape who people are and what they think they can do and be' (McLean et al. 2013, 34) in respect of primary and secondary education in schools in England. What individuals do in schools in England, produces what Bernstein (2000) refers to as a relationship between inner consciousness and the outside world of structures and systems. This 'opens up or closes down the possibilities for living' in respect of their education (McLean et al. 2013, 34) and is referred to by Bernstein (2000) as a code that represents 'embedded dispositions' and 'puts restraints on thinking feeling and action' (McLean et al. 2013, 34). In Bernstein's (2000) work, education is shaped by 'classification' and 'framing'. 'Classification' reveals power relations in society, by establishing boundaries between categories ('agents, agencies, discourses, practices' [McLean et al. 2013, 34]). In exemplifying this Bernsteinian concept, there are 'high status' and 'low status' schools in England. In Bernstein's (2000) work, framing regulates 'how knowledge, skills, and dispositions are taught and learned' (McLean et al. 2013, 34). In this chapter, Bernstein's (2000) work is applied in order to explore what is being taught, how it is being taught, and how this frames the organisational culture of schools in England.

The theoretical content in the chapter is also informed by the work of Randall and Downie (1996). As noted in the introduction to the chapter, it is argued by Randall and Downie (1996) that a medical model of thought has come to dominate understandings of health, care, and education in England. The consequence of this emphasis on the Quadrivium has led to the dominance of Hippocratic understandings of health, care, and education in England, where it is believed that 'solution A' can be applied in order to resolve 'problem B'. It appears to be the case that there is a wish to apply a magic bullet in order to cure the perceived ailments within health, care, and education in England (Urban 2009). Randall and Downie (1996) argue that the emphasis that is being placed on Hippocrates occurs to the detriment of the Asclepian notion of healing. Healing is more associated with a subjective and impressionistic Trivium. In contrast, a focus on results and targets can produce a sense of tunnel-vision through an obsessive emphasis being placed on end products (Urban 2009). If the achievement of results dominates a school's zeitgeist, it is likely that the main curriculum objective will be to focus on this objective. Enabling what Kennedy (2005, 237) refers to as a broader sense of 'transformative professional development' through focusing on other aspects of education (for example pastoral work and creativity) is less likely. This theoretical theme is applied within the chapter.

Vermunt (2016) argues that we ought to use research findings in education in ways that are similar to the black boxes of aeroplanes. In other words, research in education is about listening to hidden conversations once they are made known. Vermunt's (2016) work can be used to develop the concept that classrooms in primary and secondary schools in England are liminal environments in which interaction is created through the negotiated meanings of teachers and students. This is revealed in the work of Coffield (2006a), and Gibb (1987, 1997), in their exploration of the presence or absence of enterprise (or creativity) in education in schools. In this chapter it is asked: are the primary and secondary schools in England characterised by inventive and creative approaches to the curriculum or not? Alongside reflecting on this question, the theoretical content of the chapter considers whether or not the school leaders in the primary and secondary schools in England are akin to the Platonic kings who are associated with Coffield's (2006b) work. In the subsequent section of the chapter, key research findings about primary and secondary schools in England are highlighted in view of the theoretical themes that have been introduced and amplified thus far in the chapter.

Key Research Findings on Neoliberalism and School Education

Three of the key research findings that are focused on in this section of the chapter are:

1. Neoliberalism in England has resulted in an overemphasis being placed upon achieving outstanding educational results in primary and secondary schools in England.
2. There are tensions between the educators and the neoliberal policy-makers over which pedagogical approaches ought to be applied in primary and secondary schools in England
3. There is less emphasis being placed upon the importance of creativity within the primary and secondary school curricula.

1. Neoliberalism in England and the overemphasis being placed upon achieving outstanding educational results in primary and secondary schools in England.

A major consequence of neoliberalism in schools in England has resulted in what Perryman et al. (2011, 179) refer to as 'the pressures to deliver'. It is argued that there is a preoccupation with achievement, especially in respect of public examinations in the secondary schools in England. The education that is taking place in the secondary schools in England appears to witness what are referred to as 'a plethora of strategies aimed at improving results' (Perryman et al. 2011, 179). Moreover, these interventions are aimed at improving the position of the schools within national league tables that rank schools according to their academic achievement as evidenced in the public examinations. It is argued that these league tables have become perceived as being so important that particular schools are characterised by 'inventive, even dubious strategies to boost their performance in these tables' (Perryman et al. 2011, 180). It is of interest that this inventiveness reveals that neoliberal policies appear to influence different individuals in schools in different ways as 'policies work in and on schools in complex ways' (Perryman et al. 2011, 193). This experience of divergence within the secondary school contexts in England is interpreted by Perryman et al. as being complicated and the 'earned autonomy' that follows from doing well in the national league tables is never static as the policy landscape is characterised by change and uncertainty. The consequence of this volatile neoliberal policy landscape results in particular academic disciplines either winning or losing favour according to Formby and Wolstenholme (2012). In consequence, PSHE (Personal, Social, Health and Economic) education has become relegated in importance in secondary schools as a result of the emphasis that is being placed on attainment (Formby and Wolstenholme 2012). The delivery of PSHE appears to occur within pedagogical environments that are considered as being 'non-specific delivery models' (Formby and Wolstenhome 2012, 19) and this results in this subject area being regarded as being inferior in comparison to disciplines that are viewed as being particularly important in respect of improving performance in the national league tables. This ultimately leads to the appearance of tensions between competing pedagogical agendas, in other words 'the quest for attainment and academic results, and the quest for (supporting) wellbeing' (Formby and Wolstenhome 2012, 21). Caldwell (2010, 52) argues that this emphasis that is placed on what is phrased as 'high-stakes test-driven accountability' requires thought so that 'an alternative future' can be realised in school education in order to engender a sense of 'innovation, creativity, and passion'. It is argued by Caldwell (2010) that the high-stakes, test-driven curriculum is likely to become evident within other neoliberal cultural educational contexts over time and that the emphasis that is being placed on testing and accountability is inextricably linked to the relegation in importance of the arts, with its associated innovation, and creativity.

2. There are tensions between the educators and the neoliberal policy-makers over which pedagogical approaches ought to be applied in primary and secondary schools in England.

The emphasis that is being placed on achieving successful examination results in primary and secondary schools in England also appears to be having an impact on the sort of teaching approaches that are favoured by the neoliberal policymakers. As opposed to focusing on the teachers and their pedagogy, there is a move towards assessing the whole of the class and their learning. The previous emphasis on teachers who were akin to being like sages on stages appears to have changed into an ideal view of teaching as a process of pedagogy that engages all of the learners in working towards particular learning objectives. This argument is evident in the work of Leaton Gray and Whitty (2010) where it is acknowledged that there have been changes in models of teaching professionalism under neoliberal governments. This change to the role of the teacher is regarded as having been critically affected in England by the New Labour governments that were in power in the United Kingdom from 1997–2010. The consequence of this neoliberal intervention in teaching has been to make conceptualisations of the role of the teacher 'more structured and more formalised' (Leaton Gray and Whitty 2010, 2). In evidencing the role of neoliberal policymakers on this aspect of pedagogy in the schools, Leaton Gray and Whitty (2010) argue that teaching in England is particularly influenced by government policy objectives. In England this has witnessed the introduction of a plethora of teaching roles that vary in respect of their diversity. There are Classroom Teachers; Higher Level Teaching Assistants; Teach First trainees; and Advanced Skills Teachers. This diversification of the professional roles of teachers in England has been enabled by neoliberal policymakers and the consequence appears to be tension in respect of the accepted role and model that teachers are ideally supposed to follow. The move away from the perception of a sage on the stage appears to have resulted in the acceptance of the importance of a teacher being akin to being a facilitator of learning, or a guide on the side. Moreover, Yandell and Turvey (2007) reveal that these competing understandings of the role of teaching staff are also complicated through diverse perceptions about the ideal nature of teaching practice. Is the role of the teacher to meet professional standards, as established by the neoliberal policymakers or is teaching and learning more about the generation of learning 'communities of practice' ? (Yandell and Turvey 2007, 533). It is argued by Yandell and Turvey (2007) that this standards-based model of teaching and learning that has been introduced into England by neoliberal policymakers is also evident in Australia, Portugal, Thailand, Brazil, China and the United States. Sachs (2010) reflects on what has emerged under neoliberalism by reflecting on the competing discourses and pedagogical identities in teaching and learning in England. The consequences of these debates about which pedagogical approaches ought to be adopted and when, appears to have ultimately resulted in competing understandings about whether or not teaching is a profession and it is argued that this has led to tensions appearing in the relationships between teaching staff and neoliberal policymakers in general (Sachs 2010).

3. There is less emphasis being placed upon the importance of creativity within the primary and secondary school curricula.

One of the consequences of the increased emphasis that is being placed upon achieving successful examination results in schools in England appears to be the relegation of importance of creativity in pedagogy in the primary and secondary school curricula. The challenges of meeting targets and achieving successful examination results can work against the development of the 'possibility thinking' that Craft et al. (2013, 2) reflect on. The irony of this occurrence appears to rest in the attempts that have been evident in policies that are designed to generate creativity within pedagogy. Craft et al. (2013) argue that in England, the creation of the NACCCE (The National Advisory Committee on Creative and Cultural Education) in 1998 under New Labour in England reveals that there has been consideration of the importance of being creative within the primary and secondary school curriculum, however, it appears to be the case that other neoliberal agendas have become dominant in education so that this aspect of pedagogy is not as influential as it could be. There is evidence that primary schools in particular in England were encouraged to offer 'a more integrated and creative curriculum' (Craft et al. 2013, 2), however, the increased emphasis that is placed upon performativity in England appears to have worked against this agenda (Ball 1998). Moreover, there is evidence that emotional stress, particularly in upper primary children in England has continued to rise and that this works against the implementation of creativity in the school curriculum (Tymms and Merrell 2007). It is argued that 'curriculum overload and the backwash of high-stakes testing' is essentially 'limiting primary practice' (Craft et al. 2013, 5). In consequence, if Tymms and Merrell (2007) are correct, the increased emotional stress that upper primary children are experiencing in schools in England is likely to impact upon their subsequent education within the secondary school curriculum. It is argued by Cremin et al. (2006) that the approaches to generating creative thinking in children need to be thought through so that this aspect of the curriculum is illuminated fully. Creativity is a complex concept and Cremin et al. (2006) reveal that there are multiple models of creativity in existence within schools and that these models of creativity are associated with and derived from a tremendous variety of disciplinary and sub-disciplinary perspectives. This in turn draws attention to the importance of thinking about the complexity of being creative and generating thinking that is innovative and educational in the sense of bringing learners out of established perspectives so that they consider the world in new and imaginative ways. However, in view of the constraints that appear to exist within the curriculum that are highlighted by Tymms and Merrell (2007), the challenge of enabling creative pedagogy is considerable in schools in England. Moreover, Hassler et al. (2015) reveal that there can be a lack of coherent connection between the resources that are present to develop pedagogy within schools and the associated philosophy of pedagogy that is underpinning the development of creative thinking. This combination of a focus on performativity and results alongside an underdevelopment of creative pedagogy appears to be a significant characteristic of education within the primary and secondary schools in England.

Concluding Discussion

The research findings from Caldwell (2010), Formby and Wolstenholme (2012) and Perryman et al. (2011) reveal that neoliberalism has resulted in an overemphasis being placed upon achieving outstanding educational results in primary and secondary schools. Moreover, what can be quantified and measured seems to have become the educational zeitgeist in England and in explaining the occurrence of this aspect of schools' culture, the work of Bernstein is helpful (2000). Bernstein (2000) reveals why there is an emphasis being placed on achieving successful examination results in schools in England in consequence of neoliberalism, as the importance of measuring achievement and attainment alongside the quantification of performance has emerged to become a dominant discourse (Bernstein 2000). As noted in the earlier section of the chapter, Bernstein's (2000) concepts of 'classification' and 'framing' are helpful in understanding what is happening in primary and secondary schools in England. For Bernstein (2000), 'classification' denotes the manifestation of power relations within societies via agents, agencies, discourses, and practices (McLean et al. 2013). The socio-political and economic agendas of neoliberalism are influencing education in England and this is shaping schools' organisational characteristics (Ingleby 2015b). In exemplifying this Bernsteinian concept, the research of Caldwell (2010), Formby and Wolstenholme (2012) and Perryman et al. (2011) reveals the sense of frustration that is generated by an education system that emphasises the importance of the achievement of successful examination results over meeting the pastoral needs of students. This in turn, generates negative sentiments about the wider curriculum that is operating in the primary and secondary schools due to the educational policies of neoliberal governments. The research of Caldwell (2010), Formby and Wolstenholme (2012) and Perryman et al. (2011) is fundamentally revealing 'how knowledge, skills, and dispositions are taught and learned' (McLean et al. 2013, 34) in schools under neoliberalism. Economic and political agendas have resulted in neoliberal governments influencing schools via educational policies that are intended to monitor academic results closely through the production of league tables and this appears to 'frame' or characterise the organisational culture of primary and secondary schools in England. This in turn can work against the development of a full curriculum in which the physical, intellectual, emotional and social needs of the students are met (Formby and Wolstenholme 2012). Moreover, what is interpreted as 'appropriate' by the neoliberal policymakers beyond the classroom is regarded as being inappropriate by the educators who are working within the schools (ATL 2017). The triumph of the Quadrivium within the curriculum (Bernstein 2000) has resulted in those subjects that are perceived as being scientific and measurable dominating the curriculum (Formby and Wolstenholme 2012). However, this has narrowed the school curriculum as the intellectual development of children in primary and secondary schools appears to take precedence over their physical, emotional, and social development (Caldwell 2010). This places the education that is occurring in primary and secondary schools in England under neoliberalism at odds with more successful forms of school education that are based on sound, coherent, educational philosophies. Frierson (2016), Lillard (2005) and O'Donnell (2013); reveal that in contrast to the education system that has emerged in primary and secondary schools in England under neoliberalism, the Montessori form of pedagogy is based on a nuanced application of key behaviourist, humanist, and cognitive principles of teaching and learning that enable the full development of children. Perhaps it is the absence of pedagogical philosophy within neoliberalism in England that is resulting in the educational emphases that Caldwell (2010), Formby and Wolstenholme (2012) and Perryman et al. (2011) critique?

Leaton Gray and Whitty (2010), Sachs (2010) and Yandell and Turvey (2007); identify that are tensions between the educators and the policy-makers over which pedagogical approaches ought to be applied in primary and secondary schools in England. This research links to the work of Randall and Downie (1996) where it is argued that the power of the medical profession has become so dominant in England that it is also shaping understandings of education. Hippocrates is regarded as being a dominant influencing figure within the discourse that is occurring about education, with the associated mantra that 'problem a can be cured by solution b' (Randall and Downie 1996). In consequence, educators become visualised as being akin to professionals who exist to solve problems (Urban 2009). Randall and Downie (1996) contrast the magic bullet approach of Hippocrates by reflecting on the alternative characteristics of Asclepius, the Greek god of healing, who is opposed to curing. Healing is perceived as being more complex than curing and the healing process corresponds to what Schwandt (2005, cited in Urban 2009) refers to as the messiness of human life. It is argued by Urban (2009) that the paradigmatic view, of 'solving problems' is also related to the emphasis that is placed on achieving successful results. The philosophy of Hippocrates is an ally of the focus that is placed on achievement and attainment within educational processes (Randall and Downie 1996). The healing process places a priority upon the importance of professionals collaborating together with those they are working with to bring about a change over time by reflecting on the everyday processes that are occurring. In contrast, curing is characterised by the wish to fire a magic bullet at a problem so that it is obliterated from sight. The discourse about teachers in schools in England appears to challenge the fundamental understanding of the role of teachers (Sachs 2010). The emphasis that is placed upon the need to solve problems likewise has generated a focus on end products as opposed to concentrating on the processes that are occurring within pedagogy (Yandell and Turvey 2007). In consequence the educational standards as opposed to the processes that are generating these educational standards appears to have become the main focus of attention in primary and secondary schools in England under neoliberal governments (Yandell and Turvey 2007). The areas that are prioritised in primary and secondary schools in England under neoliberalism also appear to have consequences for the students and their educators in respect of their identities. Tymms and Merrell (2007) draw attention to the problems that are occurring for students in primary schools and their associated mental health and wellbeing and the focus on curing as opposed to healing appears to be exacerbating this problem. The research of Tymms and Merrell (2007) is complemented by the work of Fitsimons (2018) by the finding that the mental health problems of students who were aged 14 years in England in 2018 appear to have worsened in general. It appears unlikely that an emphasis being placed upon teachers as solvers of problems, who cure as opposed to heal, will help in view of these challenges, and the image of an ideal teacher who exists to meet targets appears to be creating tensions between neoliberal policymakers and educators in primary and secondary schools in England.

The research findings also reveal that less emphasis is being placed upon the importance of creativity within the primary and secondary school curricula in England. This is an aspect of the organisational culture of primary and secondary schools under neoliberalism that relates to the work of Coffield (2006a), Gibb (1987, 1997) and Guilford (1967). The consequence of focusing on results and attainment and the generation of a narrow curriculum appears to have resulted in enterprise and thinking in creative ways becoming less apparent within the curricula of the primary and the secondary schools in England. This again appears to relate back to the philosophy of education that is present within neoliberalism. The focus that is given to end products appears to remove an emphasis being placed upon the educational processes. Perhaps if neoliberal policymakers in England were to learn about effective education in primary and secondary schools, they should spend time consulting the research that has been completed on successful philosophies of pedagogy? Alongside the Montessori methods of pedagogy there is also the Reggio Emilia approach to teaching and learning. Once more, the emphasis appears to be placed on informing pedagogy via behaviourist, humanist, and cognitive principles so that there is a form of education that is based on holism (Dodd-Nufrio 2011). This appears to place the pedagogy on sound foundations. The Reggio Emilia approach to pedagogy develops what are referred to as the hundred languages of children (Edwards et al. 2012). In exploring cognitive pedagogical tasks there is an acknowledgement of the cognitive pedagogy of Vygotsky, and this systematic application of a clear sense of the purpose of the curriculum appears to generate an effective form of education. This chapter has revealed that in England in the primary and secondary schools there are interventions occurring by neoliberal policy makers that are not based on sound pedagogical philosophies. Perhaps it might be best for the neoliberal policymakers in education in England to go back to the basics?

REFERENCES

Association of Teachers and Lecturers (ATL). 2017. Accessed October 3, 2018. https://www.atl.org.uk/latest/atl-survey-finds-support-staff-increasingly-having-teach-lessons.

Ball, S. 1998. Performativity and fragmentation in the education economy: Towards the performative society? *Australian Educational Researcher* 27 (2): 1–23.

———. 2010. New class inequalities in education. Why education policy may be looking in the wrong place! Education policy, civil society and social class. *International Journal of Sociology and Social Policy* 30 (3–4): 155–166.

Bernstein, B. 2000. *Pedagogy, symbolic control and identity.* Lanham, MD: Rowman and Littlefield.

Caldwell, B.J. 2010. The impact of high-stakes test-driven accountability. *Professional Voice* 8 (1): 49–55.

Clarke, P. 2014. *Report into allegations concerning Birmingham schools arising from 'Trojan Horse' letter.* London: HMSO.

Coffield, F. 2006a. From the decade of enterprise culture to the decade of the TECs. *British Journal of Education and Work* 4 (1): 59–78.

———. 2006b. *Running ever faster down the wrong road,* Inaugural Lecture. London: London University Institute of Education.

Colmer, K., M. Waniganayake, and L. Field. 2015. Implementing curriculum reform: Insights into how Australian early childhood directors view professional development and learning. *Professional Development in Education* 41 (2): 203–221.

Craft, A., T. Cremin, P. Burnard, T. Dragovic, and K. Chappell. 2013. Possibility thinking: Culminative studies of an evidence based concept driving creativity? *International Journal of Primary, Elementary and Early Years Education* 41 (5): 3–13.

Cremin, T., P. Burnard, and C. Craft. 2006. Pedagogy and possibility thinking in the early years. *Thinking Skills and Creativity* 1 (2): 108–119.

Dodd-Nufrio, A.T. 2011. Reggio Emilia, Maria Montessori, and John Dewey: Dispelling teachers' misconceptions and understanding theoretical foundations. *Early Childhood Education Journal* 39 (1): 235–237.

Edwards, C., L. Gandini, and G. Forman. 2012. *The hundred languages of children: The Reggio Emilia experience in transformation.* Greenwich, CT: Ablex.

Fitsimons, E. 2018. *Initial findings from the MCS age 14 sweep.* Swindon: ESRC.

Formby, E., and C. Wolstenholme. 2012. 'If there's going to be a subject that you don't have to do...' Findings from a mapping study of PSHE education in English secondary schools. *Journal of Pastoral Care* 30 (1): 5–18.

Frierson, P.R. 2016. Making room for children's autonomy: Maria Montessori's case for seeing children's incapacity for autonomy as an external failing. *Journal of Philosophy of Education* 50 (3): 332–350.

Gibb, A.A. 1987. Enterprise culture- its meaning and application for education and training. *Journal of European Industrial Training* 11 (2): 38–38.

———. 1997. Enterprise culture and education. Understanding enterprise education and its links with small business, entrepreneurship, and wider educational goals. *International Small Business Journal: Researching Entrepreneurship* 11 (3): 11–34.

Glatter, R. 2012. Persistent preoccupations: The rise and rise of school accountability in England. *Educational Management Administration and Leadership* 40 (5): 559–575.

Guilford, J.P. 1967. Creativity: Yesterday, today and tomorrow. *The Journal of Creative Behaviour* 1: 3–14.

Gunter, H. 2011. *Leadership and the reform of education.* Bristol: Policy Press.

Hassler, B., L. Major, and S. Hennessy. 2015. Tablet use in schools: A critical review of the evidence for learning outcomes. *Journal of Computer Assisted Learning* 32 (2): 139–156.

Ilham, N., J.K. Kidd, M.S. Burns, and T. Campbell. 2015. Head start classroom teachers' and assistant teachers' perception of professional development using a LEARN framework. *Professional Development in Education* 41 (2): 344–365.

Ingleby, E. 2015a. The impact of changing policies about technology on the professional development needs of early years educators in England. *Professional Development in Education* 41 (1): 144–158.

———. 2015b. The house that Jack built: Neoliberalism, teaching in higher education and the moral objections. *Teaching in Higher Education* 20 (5): 507–518.

Kennedy, A. 2005. Models of CPD: A framework for analysis. *Journal of In-service Education* 31 (2): 235–250.

Leaton Gray, S.L., and G. Whitty. 2010. Social trajectories or disrupted identities? Changing and competing models of teacher professionalism under new labour. *Cambridge Journal of Education* 40 (1): 5–23.

Lillard, A. 2005. *Montessori: The science behind the genius.* Oxford: Oxford University Press.

Machin, S., and K. Salvanes. 2010. *Valuing school quality via school choice reform.* London: Centre for the Economics of Education.

Machin, S., and J. Vernoit. 2011. *Changing school autonomy: Academy schools and their introduction to England's education.* London: Centre For The Economics of Education.

Marklund, L. 2015. Preschool teachers' informal online professional development in relation to educational use of tablets in Swedish preschools. *Professional Development in Education* 41 (2): 236–253.

McCrone, T., C. Southcott, and N. George. 2011. *Governance models in schools: Local government education and children's services.* Slough: NFER.

McLean, M., A. Abbas, and P. Ashwin. 2013. A Bernsteinian view of learning and teaching undergraduate sociology-based social science. *Enhancing Learning in the Social Sciences* 5 (2): 32–44.

National Audit Office. 2017. Accessed April 12, 2017. http://www.nao.org.uk.

O'Donnell, M. 2013. *Maria Montessori: A critical introduction to key themes and debates.* London: Continuum.

Perryman, J., S. Ball, M. Maguire, and A. Braun. 2011. Life in the pressure cooker-school league tables in English and mathematics teachers' responsibilities in a results driven era. *British Journal of Educational Studies* 59 (2): 179–195.

Randall, F., and R.S. Downie. 1996. *Palliative care ethics: A good companion (Oxford Medical Publications).* Oxford: Oxford University Press.

Sachs, J. 2010. Teacher professional identity: Competing discourses, competing outcomes. *Journal of Education Policy* 16 (2): 149–161.

Schwandt, T.A. 2005. *A diagnostic of scientifically based research for education.* Malden, MA: Blackwell.

Selwyn, N. 2011. The place of technology in the conservative-Liberal democrat education agenda: An ambition of absence? *Educational Review* 63 (4): 395–408.

Tymms, P., and C. Merrell. 2007. *Standards and quality in English primary schools over time: The national evidence (primary review survey 4/1).* Cambridge: University of Cambridge Faculty of Education.

Urban, M. 2009. Strategies for change: rethinking professional development to meet the challenges of diversity in the early years profession. Paper presented at the IPDA conference, 27–28 November, Birmingham, UK.

Vermunt, J.D. 2016. Keynote address. Paper presented at the IPDA conference, 25–26 November, Stirling, UK.

Yandell, J., and A. Turvey. 2007. Standards or communities of practice? Competing models of workplace learning and development. *British Educational Research Journal* 33 (4): 533–540.

CHAPTER 4

Neoliberalism, Secondary and Tertiary Education

Introduction

This chapter explores the consequences of the neoliberal introduction of academy schools in England for FE. It is argued that the uncertain remit of the academy schools has indirect consequences for FE and that the employability agenda of the sector is challenged by the academy schools. This appears to be happening because of years of neoliberal government neglect of the FE sector in England. The chapter applies the work of the French philosopher Jean Baudrillard (1983, 1993) by arguing that the academy schools are simulating the FE agenda. In simulation, a model of reality precedes what is real. The uncertainty surrounding the exact purpose of the academy schools appears to enable them to adopt agendas that have been traditionally associated with other sectors of education. This original argument forms the basis of the new knowledge in the chapter. It is argued that the academy schools in England are a classic example of neoliberal educational policy. The schools are based on the objective of encouraging independence, so that the statutory and private sectors of education work together collectively. This objective is realized by insisting that the schools manage themselves in respect of budgets and the curriculum, like independent organisations. This is once again a simplistic oversight of the complexity that is present in forms of education and the policy of encouraging academy schools appears to be creating tension across

E. Ingleby, *Neoliberalism Across Education*, Palgrave Studies on Global Policy and Critical Futures in Education, https://doi.org/10.1007/978-3-030-73962-1_4

diverse sectors of education. In the chapter it is argued that alongside evidencing tension between policymakers and educators, neoliberalism appears to generate conflict across spheres of education.

Academy schools are able to have an impact on FE because this sector of education is accurately described by Hayes (2007) as being akin to the tale of 'Cinderella'. This analogy is used by Hayes (2007) to highlight the lack of care and consideration of FE in England by successive neoliberal governments. However, the neglect of the FE sector under neoliberalism has enabled other 'suitors' to take advantage of this educational situation (Burton et al. 2012) and this has provided the academy schools in England with opportunities. As outlined in the previous chapter, the academy schools are based on principles of self-regulation (Machin and Vernoit 2011) and this provides flexibility in terms of the agendas that the academy schools can develop. The lack of financial support for the FE sector that has resulted in its 'Cinderella' status (Creasy 2013) appears to have led to the poaching of agendas that were once the preserve of FE by the academy schools in England. Although schools in England are involved in developing employability skills in general, the academy schools are able to become part of this agenda in dynamic ways. In explaining this occurrence, the chapter applies the work of Baudrillard (Baudrillard 1983, 1993; Gane 2000; Lane 2000). Baudrillard's (1983, 1993) concept of 'simulacra' is developed in order to argue that the academy schools are able to introduce educational initiatives as a direct consequence of the uncertainty that surrounds their purpose (Clarke 2014). Baudrillard (1983) considers the importance of signs and images within societies that are described as being late modern. The basis of Baudrillard's thesis is that the social world of the West has moved beyond a tangible material reality and into something else. It is argued by Baudrillard (1983, 1993) that the signs that exist within this late modern world have become transformed so that they have acquired a potent ability to shape the world. Baudrillard (1983) reveals this argument by exemplifying 'Disneyland'. It is argued that this fantasy world of imaginary stories, moral tales and cartoon images has become a form of life in itself. The example of Disneyland is used by Baudrillard (1983) to reveal the occurrence of scripts and pictures that blur the boundaries of what is real and what is imaginary. In this chapter it is argued that the poaching of educational agendas by the academy schools in England under neoliberalism is an example of educational simulation. The agendas are not just copied or adopted. They become a fundamental part of the identity of the academy schools in a hyperreal way, to the detriment of the FE sector. This links back to Kant's question: 'How am I to develop the sense of freedom in spite of the restraint?' (Schaffar 2014, 5). The academy schools are not free as they are bound by the political and economic restraints of neoliberalism. However, it is argued in this chapter that nonetheless, the academy schools are still able to simulate agendas that once appeared to be the preserve of other sectors of education in England, despite this restraint.

Defining education is not easy as educational processes often involve complex component parts. If we go back to the Latin origins of the word education, we may see its purpose as enabling individuals to move beyond their current understanding of the world so that existence is considered in new and different ways. However, Schaffar (2014, 6) reveals that tensions can exist between 'educational influence' and 'child development' and that the definition of education can become a pedagogical paradox. This paradox is described by Peters (1963) as being the tension that exists between enabling autonomy alongside limiting choices in those who are being educated. In consequence a key element in defining education is to consider whether or not it is possible to be neutral in our work as educators. The implication is that an absence of neutrality restricts child development as revealed in Kant's concern over the relationship between free will and education (Schaffar 2014) and this theme is also considered within the work of Kateb (2011), Krek (2015), and Li (2018). This discussion of education and its purpose is explored in the pedagogy of Montessori, Reggio Emilia and Steiner and is referenced in the work of Kauder and Fischer (1999), Luckner (2003), and Ruhloff (1975). Vanderstraeten and Biesta (2001, 10) argue that Kant has identified a key educational problem in exploring a 'definition of man and his destination'. Moreover, both Heidegger (1996) and Gadamer (1990) also reflect on the importance of enabling individuals to develop a sense of community through becoming educated (Schaffar 2014). However, the challenge for educationalists is revealed by Biesta (2006) in the argument that pedagogy is intimately linked to political and economic agendas. In the subsequent sections of this chapter it is argued that the political and economic agendas of neoliberalism shape the two educational contexts that are explored (academy schools and FE). Education is not just about enabling individuals to see the world in different ways because defining education in England necessitates considering the political and economic factors that define neoliberalism and subsequently impact on forms of education.

SCHOOLS AND FE

The content of the previous chapters has referred to academy schools and it has been argued that this type of school is a form of educational environment that provokes debate (Machin and Vernoit 2011). This is because the schools are 'independent, non-selective, state funded and outside the control of local authorities' (Machin and Vernoit 2011, 2). As revealed in Chap. 3, the management of the schools occurs from an independent team of sponsors and a predominantly self-appointed group of governors (Machin and Vernoit 2011, 2) who are able to influence the school and its curriculum in new and unconventional ways (Ball 2010; Caldwell and Harris 2008; Clarke 2014; Glatter 2013; Greany and Scott 2014; Gunter 2011; Hatcher 2011; Machin and Salvanes 2010; Machin and Vernoit 2011; McCrone et al. 2011). In this chapter it is argued that the uncertain and flexible arrangement within the academy schools allows for the simulation of agendas that have been traditionally the preserve of other sectors of education in England. In particular, it is argued that the academy schools are able to simulate an employability agenda that has been previously regarded as a key part of the work of the FE sector in England. However, in developing this argument it is important to note that the academy schools are not imitating the FE sector. This is because simulation is occurring due to the explicit message that is given that the academy schools are the best place for employability needs to be met. In the chapter it is argued that this is an unforeseen consequence of years of neglect of the FE sector in England by successive neoliberal governments.

In England, the FE sector is experiencing significant challenges (Tummons and Ingleby 2014, 59). The sector is characterised by varied types of educational institution that are offering numerous types of educational programmes. Tummons and Ingleby (2014) apply the Geertzian (1988, 2) phrase 'Heraclitus cubed and worse' in referring to the constant change that characterises this sector of English education. What was once referred to as 'further education' became known as the 'learning and skills sector'. The sector is now referred to as 'the lifelong learning sector' (Tummons and Ingleby 2014, 59), and the changes that have always happened in the sector appear to mirror the complexity of the learners (Tummons and Ingleby 2014, 59). Earlier in the chapter, the Hayes' (2007) description of the sector resembling 'Cinderella' was used as a metaphor to represent the vulnerability of this educational context and it can be argued that this 'neglect' has occurred over a number of years. In exploring the complexity of FE in England, The Wolf Report, commissioned in 2011 reveals the variable quality of vocational education in England (Tummons and Ingleby 2014, 155) and the report makes three key points (Tummons and Ingleby 2014, 156). The unsatisfactory achievement of young people aged 14–19 years in England in English and mathematics is noted as being problematic; the curriculum is described as being sclerotic, rigid and unresponsive; and vocational education is regarded as being 'expensive and overly-centralised' (Tummons and Ingleby 2014, 156). The curriculum is portrayed as having too many awarding bodies and too many qualifications and this failing curriculum in FE in England is portrayed by The Wolf Report 2011 as being wholly unsatisfactory. In view of this failing provision of vocational education, due to the neglect of successive neoliberal English governments (Atkins 2013), it is argued in this chapter that the academy schools are presented with opportunities. As newly created educational institutions, they are able to make vocational education a key part of their remit. This is possible due to the deregulation of the academy schools (Machin and Vernoit 2011). Hatcher (2011) refers to the free schools that are enabled within the academy school system and in the chapter it is argued that this autonomy of the academy schools that is noted by Glatter (2012, 2013) provides them with opportunities to challenge the FE agenda in England.

Theoretical Background

The research findings in the chapter are considered alongside the work of Baudrillard (1983, 1993). Gane (2000) argues that three connected theses of Baudrillard are of interest to social scientists. The first thesis proposes that Western culture has established interpretations of 'the real world' (Gane 2000, 34). The existence of a variety of educational contexts in England exemplifies this argument, as the 'real world of English education' is constituted of pre-school, primary, secondary, College and University educational contexts. The second thesis of Baudrillard's (1983, 1993) work explores what Gane (2000) refers to as an exaggeration of the real world. In Western cultures we experience 'a simulation of the real that is taken to extremes' (Lane 2000, 86). This is revealed in examples of 'hyperreality' (Gane 2000, 34). Baudrillard's (1983) portrayal of hyperreality is described by Gane (2000, 95) as being 'bleak', as the hyperreal is a product of governments and media groups so hyperreality is accordingly tainted and never utopian. In exemplifying this argument, it can be argued that the academy schools and FE Colleges in England exist beyond their physical boundaries. However, academy schools and FE Colleges share identities with other educational organisations despite being distinct educational spaces, as they operate within a collective national education sector and the consequence of the existence of shared educational contexts connects educational organisations together. This hyperreal nature of the academy schools and FE Colleges in England is a consequence of the government policies that have formed the institutions (Gane 2000, 34). Baudrillard's (1983, 1993) third thesis proposes that there is a complex manifestation of the real in Western cultures. What is real can become 'virtual' as a consequence of a 'shattering into fractal dimensions' (Gane 2000, 34). Baudrillard's (1993) philosophical approach is partly influenced by Nietzsche in its exploration of human 'will'. It can also be argued that Baudrillard (1983, 1993) is influenced by the philosophy of Plato and Kant (Audi 1995). There is an exploration of complex, big questions within the work of Baudrillard. Just as Plato evidences a quest for answers to big questions (to exemplify for example, 'what is love?') so Baudrillard investigates the broader implications of his three lines of philosophical enquiry. Alongside this wider focus, Baudrillard's (1983, 1993) work also evidences the influence of Kant due to the interest in what Audi (1995, 400) phrases as a 'Copernican revolution' of thought through also focusing on smaller questions. Kant's question 'How am I to develop the sense of freedom in spite of the restraint?' (Schaffar 2014, 5) is similar to part of Baudrillard's (1983, 1993) line of philosophical enquiry. In consequence Baudrillard's (1983, 1993) work is associated with a philosophical trend acknowledging the forces that are shaped by individuals, alongside an imaginary discursively constructed world that is beyond the remit of mere individuals.

Baudrillard's (1983, 1993) philosophy is applied to the chapter to explain what is happening within the academy schools in England. It is argued that the academy schools are simulating the FE agenda. There is the exemplification of what Baudrillard (1983, 1993) refers to as 'a third order of simulation' (Gane 2000, 86). With a first order of simulation there is a representation of what is real. A diary reflection by a teacher in an academy school is an example of a first order simulation. The diary reflection provides an account of what it is like to be a teacher in an academy school. This diary reflection, however, is not the same as actually being a teacher in an academy school. A second order simulation occurs when the division between reality and representation becomes blurred

(Baudrillard 1983). Baudrillard (1983) exemplifies this form of second order simulation with maps. A map of an academy school is such an exact representation of the educational context that the map and the place exist in tandem. They become as real as each other. However, with a third order simulation, the model precedes reality (Gane 2000). There occurs a separation of what is real from what is simulated. In this chapter it is argued that this is happening in academy schools in England. There is not an imitation of the FE agenda of developing employability skills. An employability agenda has emerged to become part of the remit of the academy schools in a way that is hyperreal. The academy schools are perceived to be free to do whatever they wish to do (within reason) and this in turn precedes their actual identity (Hatcher 2011). This accounts for why the academy schools are able to make employability agendas such a key part of their identity. Gane (2000, 98) explains hyperreality in this instance with an analogy. When we get too close to an object it is difficult to distinguish what the object is. Hyperreality is like a close-up and a long-distance photograph at the same time. There is, therefore, no third normative realistic perspective as a fake existence occurs in the sense of the representation blurring with the real.

KEY RESEARCH FINDINGS

The research findings on academy schools reveals three key findings:

1. Academy schools are regarded as having a responsibility for nurturing employability skills.
2. At policy level, academy schools are regarded as being responsible for developing employability skills in novel, dynamic ways.
3. Academy schools are regarded as being servants of the local community.

This section of the chapter amplifies these three research themes.

1. Academy schools are regarded as having a responsibility for nurturing employability skills.

One of the interesting features of the academy schools in England is their perceived responsibility for ensuring that employability skills are nurtured in students. Woods et al. (2007, 237) refer to the 'entrepreneurial features' of the academy schools in England in their research on 58 academy schools. It is argued that the academy schools are 'intended to enhance the growing influence of private versions of entrepreneurialism' (Woods et al. 2007, 237) and in consequence this places the development of employability skills high on their educational agenda. The creation of 'trust' status for the academy schools appears to have enabled a flexibility that facilitates the schools to make the development of employability skills a key part of their remit. It is also argued by Woods et al. (2007) that the philosophy that rests behind the academy schools is based on enabling them to become more entrepreneurial and more innovative and that essentially this can be traced back to their ethos in that the schools are independently managed and sponsored. The flexibility of the focus of the academy schools is also possible because they are able to 'play a key part in the regeneration of communities' (Woods et al. 2007, 238). The autonomous nature of the academy schools means that they are different to the traditional schools in England (Eyles and Machin 2019). It is argued by Eyles and Machin (2019, 1108) that the schools were introduced in part due to an anxiety from the neoliberal New Labour government that 'the teachers had lost the control of the corridors' and the new academy school structure is based on the management of the school by a private team of independent co-sponsors. In giving power back to educators, if the teachers and the school sponsors wish to focus on developing the employability skills of the students, it is argued that they are enabled to do this. Salokangas and Chapman (2014) reveal that the policy and practice of multi-academy chains where a number of academy schools are amalgamated together, heightens the power of the academy schools in respect of focusing on particular agendas like employability. The intensity and boldness of the reform to the schools is likened to 'a real life laboratory' with respect to the governance of the schools and the agendas they are able to develop (Salaokangas and Chapman 2011, 372).

Purcell (2014, 49) refers to the 'discourse of aspiration' that characterises the agendas of the academy schools in general. It is argued by Purcell (2014) that the academy schools were introduced with the intention of providing hope for communities that are disadvantaged and it is also argued that diversity and choice are two of the key themes that characterise the agenda of the academy schools. Purcell (2014) reveals that the discourses regarding aspirations; opportunities; and attainment are especially apparent in the discussions about the academies programme and these three themes are highly relevant to employability agendas. Moreover, these discourses appear to change over time with 'academic performance being linked to low aspirations' and subsequently to 'a low ethos' (Purcell 2014, 53). It is also argued by Purcell (2014, 54) that the 'absence of opportunity' is in turn associated with 'the absence of educational attainment' so that performance and opportunity and employability are associated with each other as part of an evolving discourse that emerges with the introduction of the academy schools in view of their perceived flexibility and freedom from constraint. In particular, the academy schools are regarded as being able to provide opportunities for the future, by equipping people with the skills that they need so they are in turn able to subsequently work in the knowledge economy and this reveals the key aim of developing the skills of employability that appears as a central objective of the academy schools (Purcell 2014). Purcell (2014) reveals that the discourse that is associated with the academy schools is characterised by the ability to transform the life chances for the next generation so that the opportunities are improved for children. Moreover Purcell (2014, 54) argues that these discourses about standards, opportunities, and aspirations in respect of the development of employability skills are utterly dependent upon the construction of the portrayal of the predecessor schools as being 'poorly performing, offering few opportunities, with low expectations'. It can be argued that this discourse is being used to generate an image of the academy schools in hyperreal ways. This is because, as Purcell (2014, 59) argues, 'discourses not only change over time but are repeated, reworked and contested at a local level' and the flexibility of the academy school structure enables these schools to evidence these malleable qualities. The ability to nurture employability skills appears to be a key characteristic that is associated with the academy schools in England and as Ingleby and Tummons (2017) argue, this aspect of the agenda of the academy schools is characterised by something that is far more potent than a mere wish to imitate the agenda of the FE sector in England.

2. At policy level, academy schools are regarded as being responsible for developing employability skills in novel, dynamic ways.

The perceived new and fresh approach of the academy schools (Salokangas and Chapman 2014) is considered by the neoliberal policymakers to be a platform from which employability skills can be developed in ways that are novel and dynamic. Woods et al. (2007, 238) refer to the 'third way commitment' that is evident in the academy schools in England as they are based on private principles, practices, and ways of working and the intention of this rationale is to enable innovative and entrepreneurial ways of working. The encouragement of partnership working and the inclusion of business and enterprise within the curriculum is based on what Woods et al. (2007) refer to as an entrepreneurial spirit. As well as developing employability skills in students, this role of the academy schools in England is characterised by the imperative to be 'innovative and risk-taking' (Woods et al. 2007, 238). The private sector characteristics of the academy schools include being independently managed alongside being supported by independent sponsors (DfES 2004) and this enables the academy schools to be associated with employability agendas that have been previously cited such as 'the regeneration of communities' (Woods et al. 2007, 238). Moreover, the association with employability and creative and innovative approaches to enabling this aspect of the curriculum is enhanced through the possibility of the presence of business sponsors. As Woods et al. (2007, 238) reveal, 'these private sponsors contribute up to £2 million of the capital of a new academy' and as a result of this contribution, they have ' a formal role in its governance' alongside being able to 'influence its development and ethos'. Although the academy schools are expected to offer a broad and balanced curriculum to pupils of all abilities, their freedom from the local authorities also allows them to offer specialist areas of the curriculum where they can choose a particular subject focus (Woods et al. 2007). This links to the research of Ingleby and Tummons (2017) who reveal that one of the academy schools in their research study focused on business studies and invited local employers to be part of this new innovative curriculum development in order to focus upon developing employability skills in ways that were creative and dynamic. As Woods et al. (2007, 252) argue, within the academy school ethos there is a key emphasis being placed on 'the type of skills and knowledge needed by the workers' and the nurturing of a creative and innovative curriculum that is possible by being freed from the perceived constraints of the local authorities in England.

Hill et al. (2012) argue that the presence of collaborative chains of academy schools enables innovative practice in respect of extending the scope of what the schools are able to do with each other. This is exemplified with the emergence of what are referred to as 'studio schools' for children who are aged 14–19 years in that the schools are able to deliver project-based learning that develops practical and vocational skills alongside focusing on mainstream educational activity. However, the practical reality of the policy initiative that rests behind the introduction of the academy schools in England is not necessarily a process that witnesses the realisation of creativity and effective contextualised practices (Wilkins 2017). This leads Kauko and Salokangas (2015, 1108) to argue that the innovative and creative policy visualisation of the introduction of academy schools at national level is 'not manifest at local level'. It is argued by Kauko and Salokangas (2015) that this is because the neoliberal English emphasis on inspection and testing does not facilitate an entrepreneurial approach to education, and this can be visualised as a chain of restraint that restricts the development of skills in novel and innovative ways. The challenge of realising this agenda of developing employability skills creatively is revealed in Heilbronn's (2016, 316) argument that since academy schools are based on privatised principles, 'they cannot deliver equity'. Heilbronn (216, 316) develops this argument by acknowledging that 'a privatised system by its very nature is part of a fragmented service' and in consequence 'at best' the service 'works for the good of the individual school, or cluster of schools'. Although the policy perception of the academy schools may be that they develop employability skills in innovative and creative ways, their reality in practice appears as divisive and individual as opposed to being collective and developmental.

3. Academy schools are regarded as being servants of the local community.

A key theme within the research that has been completed on academy schools concerns their responsibility for providing helpful services for the local community. Papanastasiou (2013, 452) refers to the perceived importance of having 'a very meaningful role' within the community as a main motivating reason for sponsors becoming involved with academy schools, alongside the belief that these schools are regarded as being responsible for creating 'a really sustainable community'. In serving the local areas they are situated in, the academies are associated with 'organisational values of localism and community participation' (Papanastasiou 2013, 452). Moreover, the issue of the local communities lacking the skills that are demanded by employers is considered to be an issue that needs to be addressed as academy schools develop their role in serving the local communities (Papanastasiou 2013). Chapman's (2011, 341) research reveals that the school leaders who are working in the academies acknowledge the 'unprecedented range of opportunities' that are present, and that this can be extended 'beyond their school and immediate community'. This research finding is complemented by the work of Purcell (2014, 54) who reports that the academy schools are directly involved 'with local industries' and with 'a community that has lost its reason for being'. Subsequently this 'opportunity' that can be associated with the academy schools is described as being 'positive for the children' as well as for 'the whole community' (Purcell 2014, 57).

Woods et al. (2007, 243) make reference to the 'cultural entrepreneurialism' that is associated with the academy schools. This refers to the creation of and taking up of opportunities to innovate, and this appears to be a characteristic of the academy schools. An interesting development with the creation of the academy schools is what is referred to by Woods et al. (2007, 243) as being 'a mission to bring meaning'. This cultural entrepreneurialism that is associated with the academy schools appears to be based on ensuring that 'a higher ethic' (Woods et al. 2007, 243) is associated with the academy schools so that they are fundamentally involved with responding to the needs of the local community. Some of these emphases that are being placed on responding to the needs of the local communities include 'welfare, responsiveness to and involvement of local people, working to improve the environment, participation in local regeneration and cooperation with other agencies' (Woods et al. 2007, 248). This approach to pedagogy that is occurring within the academy schools appears to place the greater needs of the local communities at the centre of the ethos of the academy schools and this results in what Woods et al. (2007, 249) refer to as the attempt to meet 'some of the complex aims inherent in advancing the public good'. This has led to one of the academy schools in the research sample of Woods et al. (2007, 250) describing itself as having a relationship with the wider community 'where each work best when they work as one, adopting democratic and inclusive decision-making governance and structures'. Woods et al. (2007) apply the work of Ball (2005) to their research by arguing that the language of community that is employed by the academy schools appears to be resulting in the construction of particular narratives about the purposes of the academy schools in England and their respective roles with the community. As Ingleby and Tummons (2017) argue this constructed discourse is based upon the academy schools in England being visualised as educational servants of their local communities.

CONCLUDING DISCUSSION

Vermunt's (2016) work has been previously cited as he argues that we need to listen to the conversations that are hidden within what he refers to as the black boxes of education. The research that has been completed on the neoliberal introduction of academy schools in England reveals that their purpose is viewed as being similar to the statements that are contained on The Association of Colleges (2016) website about the rationale for FE. The importance of developing the skills that are required by employers and the essential nature of training and vocationalism, alongside serving the community, are consistent themes that appear on this website. The research on the academy schools draws attention to the importance of ensuring that employability skills are developed in young people and these schools appear to be regarded as having the responsibility of filling the void that has been left by previously unsuccessful forms of vocational education, by providing the employability skills that are needed if young people are to be successful (Purcell 2014). The challenges within skills development are commented on within the academic community in England (for example, in the work of Bathmaker and Avis 2005), and the academy schools appear to be provided with opportunities in view of the failing tertiary sector of education that is present in England (Tummons and Ingleby 2014). The newness of the academy schools and their innovative qualities are presented as a potential antidote to the problems within the secondary education system and its emphasis that is placed on achieving high marks in exams, tests and summative assessment (Strathern 2000, cited in Ingleby and Gibby 2016). The old school curriculum can be perceived as evidencing a lack of focus on the processes of education (Ingleby 2014, 2015a; Lucas 2007, cited in Ingleby and Gibby 2016, Vermunt 2016). Moreover, the challenges facing the FE curriculum in England evidence challenges in student retention and achievement (Schofield and Dismore 2010); complexities in governance (Harwood and Harwood 2004; Trim 2001); and insufficient resourcing for pedagogy (Burkill et al. 2008; Feather 2010, 2012; Wilson and Wilson 2011; Young 2006). This tertiary sector has experienced years of neglect (Tummons and Ingleby 2014) and this accounts in part for the dim view that is taken of the development of employability skills by those completing research on this sector of education. The development of these skills may be regarded as being a 'house that Jack built' (Ingleby 2015b) and the consequences of neglecting the FE sector in England has resulted in an absence of vocational skills in young people in England (Hayes 2007). This appears to provide the academy schools with opportunities, however, as revealed by Clarke (2014), the academy schools are enigmatic and moreover as argued in this chapter, their model precedes their reality.

The research that has been completed on academy schools in England reveals a form of school that has autonomy and flexibility of governance (Ball 2010; Caldwell and Harris 2008; Glatter 2013; Greany and Scott 2014; Gunter 2011; Hatcher 2011; Machin and Salvanes 2010; Machin and Vernoit 2011; and McCrone et al. 2011). This flexibility of governance enables the schools to move into areas of education that may be unexpected, and it is possible for the academy schools to define themselves as champions of employability because of their loose structure of governance (Machin and Vernoit 2011). The autonomy of the academy schools can result in more segregation in society (Ball 2010; Clarke 2014) and as Machin and Vernoit (2011) reveal, there can be variable consequences for education in England because of the academy schools. One consequence is their ability to improve the quality of their pupil intake as a result of their autonomy (Machin and Vernoit 2011) and this flexibility is especially apparent in those schools that converted to academy status soon after their introduction in England in 2002. The research of Machin and Vernoit (2011, 46) reveals that the academy schools have 'significant beneficial effects' for the schools that are not academies as it is argued that the competition that is provided by a mixed educational system can result in improvements in educational performance. The research findings of Machin and Vernoit (2011) explain why the number of academy schools in England has increased since 2002. These schools are regarded as being an ideal form of school by the neoliberal educational policymakers in England and moreover, the academy schools appear to be dynamic educational institutions that are capable of moving into other sectors of education, like FE due to the neglect of this tertiary sector of education by neoliberal policymakers (Tummons and Ingleby 2014).

The work of Baudrillard (1983, 1993) can be applied in order to explain how academy schools are able to adopt the agendas of other educational institutions. Baudrillard (1983, 1993) is useful because his work explains the occurrence of hyperreality. In hyperreality, a model precedes what is real (Gane 2000; Lane 2000) and within the academy schools, their 'free' and 'autonomous' nature is revealed in the policy discourse about them (for example in DfES 2004). The schools may be championed by the neoliberal policymakers alongside being criticised by the educational researchers who are cited in this chapter and this discourse is based on particular interpretations of what is perceived as being real. The emotions that are generated by the discussions about academy schools (for example Clarke 2014) appear to be an example of what Lane (2000, 100) refers to as 'the society of the spectacle'. The neoliberal policymakers in England in general refer to academy schools as being fundamentally good, and yet they are critiqued by the academic researchers as being a fundamentally bad development (Glatter 2013). In this chapter it is argued that the academy schools are examples of hyperreality (Lane 2000). In hyperreality, there is not a false existence as there is the creation of another form of reality, where a model of reality precedes what is real (Baudrillard 1983, 1993; Gane 2000; Lane 2000). There is the production of a type of virtual reality that is a product of a wish about what reality should be and hyperreality occurs when this model of the real becomes enacted. This appears to be happening with the academy schools in England as the wish to have a form of school that realises neoliberal educational policy agendas appears to have become the model that the neoliberal policymakers favour. In this chapter it is argued that this model is duplicitous because the academy schools are examples of hyperreal institutions that are operating 'as a testing ground' (Lane 2000, 101) for a form of education. The flexible nature of the academy schools produces unintended consequences as the schools can adopt other educational agendas that are associated with other domains of education in England, like the FE sector. This chapter reveals that the academy schools regard employability as a key part of their remit and that the FE sector agenda is being adopted by the academy schools in England. Moreover, there is not an imitation of the FE education agenda as the model of the academy schools as free and autonomous allows these educational institutions to associate themselves with this employability agenda (Ingleby and Tummons 2017). The academy schools do not appear to possess a coherent philosophy of pedagogy as they are free and autonomous, and they are able to do whatever they wish to do within reason. Alongside this facet of the operational dynamic of the academy schools in England, the FE sector too appears to be devoid of a coherent philosophy of education and as such, the pinching of its educational identity and agendas by hyperreal neoliberal educational institutions is made possible and enabled.

REFERENCES

Atkins, L. 2013. From marginal learning to marginal employment? The real impact of learning employability skills. *Power and Education* 5 (1): 28–37.

Audi, R. 1995. *The Cambridge dictionary of philosophy*. Cambridge: Cambridge University Press.

Ball, S.J. 2005. Radical policies, progressive modernisation and deepening democracy: The academies programme in action. *Forum* 47 (2 & 3): 215–222.

Ball, S. 2010. New class inequalities in education. Why education policy may be looking in the wrong place! Education policy, civil society and social class. *International Journal of Sociology and Social Policy* 30 (3–4): 155–166.

Bathmaker, A.M., and J. Avis. 2005. Becoming a lecturer in further education in England: The construction of professional identity and the role of communities of practice. *The Journal of Education for Teaching* 31 (1): 47–62.

Baudrillard, J. 1983. *Simulations*. London: MIT Press.

———. 1993. *Symbolic exchange and death*. London: Sage.

Biesta, G.J.J. 2006. *Beyond learning. Democratic education for a human future*. Boulder, CO: Paradigm Publishers.

Burkill, S., S. Rodway-Dyer, and M. Stone. 2008. Lecturing in higher education in further education settings. *Journal of Further and Higher Education* 32 (4): 321–331.

Burton, K., M. Lloyd, and C. Griffiths. 2012. Barriers to learning for mature students studying HE in an FE college. *Journal of Further and Higher Education* 35 (1): 25–36.

Caldwell, B.J., and J. Harris. 2008. *Why not the best schools?* Camberwell: Acer Press.

Chapman, C. 2011. Academy federations, chains, and teaching schools in England: Reflections on leadership, policy, and practice. *Journal of School Choice* 7 (3): 334–352.

Clarke, P. 2014. *Report into allegations concerning Birmingham schools arising from 'Trojan Horse' letter*. London: HMSO.

Creasy, R. 2013. HE lite: Exploring the problematic position of HE in FECs. *Journal of Further and Higher Education* 37 (1): 38–53.

Department for Education and Skills. 2004. *Five year strategy for children and learners: Putting people at the heart of public services*. London: The Stationery Office.

Eyles, A., and S. Machin. 2019. The introduction of academy schools to England's education. *Journal of the European Economic Association* 17 (4): 1107–1146.

Feather, D. 2010. A whisper of academic identity: An HE in FE perspective. *Research in Post-compulsory Education* 15 (2): 189–204.

———. 2012. Do lecturers delivering higher education in further education desire to conduct research? *Research in Post-compulsory Education* 17 (3): 335–347.

Gadamer, H.-G. 1990. *Warheit und methode*. Tubingen: Mohr Siebeck.

Gane, M. 2000. *Jean Baudrillard: in radical uncertainty*. London: Pluto Press.
Geertz, C. 1988. *Works and lives: The anthropologist as author*. Stanford: Stanford University Press.
Glatter, R. 2012. Persistent preoccupations: The rise and rise of school accountability in England. *Educational Management Administration and Leadership* 40 (5): 559–575.
———. 2013. Academy schools: a flawed system that cannot be sustained. Accessed 21, July, 2016. https://www.theguardian.com/teacher-network/teacher-blog/2013/jan/24/academy-school-system-heading-rocks.
Greany, T., and J. Scott. 2014. *Conflicts of interest in academy sponsorship arrangements. A report for the education select committee*. London: Institute of Education.
Gunter, H. 2011. *Leadership and the reform of education*. Bristol: Policy Press.
Harwood, J., and D. Harwood. 2004. Higher education in further education: Delivering higher education in a further education context: A study of five south west colleges. *Journal of Further and Higher Education* 28 (2): 153–164.
Hatcher, R. 2011. Local government against local democracy: A case study. In *The state and education policy: The academy programme*, ed. H. Gunter, 39–52. London: Bloomsbury.
Hayes, D. 2007. *A lecturer's guide to further education: Inside the 'cinderella sector.* Milton Keynes: Open University Press.
Heidegger, M. 1996. *Being and time*. Albany, N.Y: State University of New York.
Heilbronn, R. 2016. Freedoms and perils: Academy schools in England. *Journal of Philosophy of Education* 50 (3): 306–318.
Hill, R., J. Dunford, N. Parish, S. Rea, and L. Sandals. 2012. *The growth of academy chains: Implications for leaders and leadership*. London: National College for School Leadership.
Ingleby, E. 2014. Developing reflective practice or judging teaching performance? The implications for mentor training. *Research in post-compulsory education* 19 (1): 18–33.
———. 2015a. The impact of changing policies about technology on the professional development needs of early years educators in England. *Professional Development in Education* 41 (1): 144–158.
———. 2015b. The house that Jack built: Neoliberalism, teaching in higher education and the moral objections. *Teaching in Higher Education* 20 (5): 507–518.
Ingleby, E., and C. Gibby. 2016. Law and ethics: Problematising the role of the foundation degree and paralegal education in English post-compulsory education. *Research in Post-compulsory Education* 21 (1–2): 151–163.
Ingleby, E., and J.E. Tummons. 2017. Imitation is not always flattery! The consequences of academy schools in England for further education policy. *Research in Post-compulsory Education* 22 (4): 237–251.
Kateb, G. 2011. *Human dignity*. Cambridge, MA: Harvard University Press.

Kauder, P., and W. Fischer. 1999. *Immanuel Kant uber pedagogik: 7 studien.* Baltmannsweiler: Schneider-Verl. Hohengehren.

Kauko, J., and M. Salokangas. 2015. The evaluation and steering of English academy schools through inspection and examinations: National visions and local practices. *British Educational Research Journal* 41 (6): 1108–1124.

Krek, J. 2015. Two principles of early moral education: A condition for the law, reflection and autonomy. *Studies in Philosophy and Education* 34: 9–29.

Lane, R.J. 2000. *Jean Baudrillard.* London: Routledge.

Li, Z. 2018. *A new approach to Kant.* Singapore: Springer.

Lucas, N. 2007. Rethinking initial teacher education for further education teachers: From a standards-led to a knowledge-based approach. *Teaching Education* 18 (2): 93–106.

Luckner, A. 2003. Erziehung zur freiheit. Immanuel Kant und die padagogik. *Padagogik* 7–8: 72–76.

Machin, S., and K. Salvanes. 2010. *Valuing school quality via school choice reform.* London: Centre for the Economics of Education.

Machin, S., and J. Vernoit. 2011. *Changing school autonomy: Academy schools and their introduction to England's education.* London: Centre For The Economics of Education.

McCrone, T., C. Southcott, and N. George. 2011. *Governance models in schools: Local government education and children's services.* Slough: NFER.

Papanastasiou, N. 2013. Commercial actors and the governing of education: The case of academy school sponsors in England. *European Educational Research Journal* 12 (4): 447–462.

Peters, R.S. 1963. Reason and habit: The paradox of moral education. In *Moral education in a changing society*, ed. W.R. Niblett, 46–65. London: Faber.

Purcell, K. 2014. Discourses of aspiration, opportunity and attainment: Promoting and contesting the academy schools programme. *Children's Geographies* 9 (1): 49–61.

Ruhloff, J. 1975. Wie kultiviere ich die freiheit bei dem zwange? *Vierteljahresschrift fur wissenschaftliche padagogik* 51: 2–18.

Salokangas, M., and C. Chapman. 2014. Exploring governance in two chains of academy schools: A comparative case study. *Educational Management Leadership and Administration* 42 (3): 372–386.

Schaffar, B. 2014. Changing the definition of education. On Kant's educational paradox between freedom and restraint. *Studies in Philosophy and Education* 33 (1): 5–21.

Schofield, C., and H. Dismore. 2010. Predictors of retention and achievement of higher education students within a further education context. *Journal of Further and Higher Education* 34 (2): 207–221.

Strathern, M., ed. 2000. *Audit cultures: Anthropological studies in accountability, ethics and the academy.* London: Routledge.

Trim, P. 2001. A review of educational partnership arrangements in further and higher education: Pointers for managers in further education. *Research in Post-compulsory Education* 6 (2): 187–203.

Tummons, J.E., and E. Ingleby. 2014. *An A-Z of the lifelong learning sector.* Maidenhead: Open University Press.

Vanderstraeten, R., and G.J.J. Biesta. 2001. How is education possible? Preliminary investigations for a theory of education. *Educational Philosophy and Theory* 33 (1): 7–21.

Vermunt, J.D. 2016. Keynote address. Paper presented at the IPDA conference, 25–26 November, Stirling, UK.

Wilkins, A. 2017. Rescaling the local: Multi-academy trusts, private monopoly and statecraft in England. *Educational Administration and History* 49 (2): 171–186.

Wilson, A., and B. Wilson. 2011. Pedagogy of the repressed: Research and professionality within HE in FE. *Research in Post-compulsory Education* 16 (4): 465–478.

Woods, A., J. Woods, and H. Gunter. 2007. Academy schools and entrepreneurialism in education. *Journal of Education Policy* 22 (2): 237–259.

Young, M. 2006. Further and higher education: Seamless or differentiated future? *Journal of Further and Higher Education* 30 (1): 1–10.

CHAPTER 5

Neoliberalism and Further Education

INTRODUCTION

This chapter considers the competing understandings of mentoring that are present within the FE sector in England. The Anderson and Shannon (1988) model of mentoring is based on a nurturing, caring, Rogerian philosophy, however this contrasts with other mentoring models (for example Daloz 1986) that are favoured by neoliberal governments and combine 'support' with 'challenge'. This latter judgemental model of mentoring can be used to try to assess the effectiveness of the educators' ability to teach and it appears to be the preferred choice of Ofsted (Lawy and Tedder 2011). The chapter considers the consequences that this choice of mentoring model is having for the FE sector in England. Mentoring is a form of pedagogy that evidences the potential for transformative experiences in teaching and learning (Kennedy 2005). However, it is argued that the processes of pedagogy are considered in particular ways by neoliberal quangos like Ofsted due to the measurement and assessment of teaching performance in FE (Ingleby 2014). In this respect, mentoring in this sector of education appears to be mirroring what is happening within the worlds of business and commerce. Performance is being assessed in this judgemental model of mentoring and this is further evidence that there is an absence of a coherent pedagogical philosophy in neoliberal interventions in education. The worlds of business and

© The Author(s), under exclusive license to Springer Nature Switzerland AG 2021
E. Ingleby, *Neoliberalism Across Education*, Palgrave Studies on Global Policy and Critical Futures in Education,
https://doi.org/10.1007/978-3-030-73962-1_5

commerce are once again influencing education and this misinterpretation of the real purpose of education appears to be one of the causes of tension and division in FE in England.

The emergence of FE mentoring has been considered by a number of authors in recent years (Hankey 2004; Ingleby 2010, 2011, 2014; Ingleby and Hunt 2008; Ingleby and Tummons 2012; Lawy and Tedder 2011; Tedder and Lawy 2009). These authors acknowledge the tensions that are present in competing understandings of mentoring in FE in England and the neoliberal policymaker preference for a model of mentoring that is judgemental. As previously acknowledged, the Anderson and Shannon (1988) model of mentoring is based on a nurturing, caring, Rogerian philosophy, and this contradicts the 'support' with 'challenge' approach of other models of mentoring. This latter judgemental model of mentoring that is as previously noted the preference of Ofsted can be used to assess professional performance (Lawy and Tedder 2011). As we have seen thus far in this book, a problematic issue with the neoliberal policymakers is made manifest in their frequent lack of practical experience in the areas that they are making policies about. Those who are working in FE often come from a variety of backgrounds, with differing levels of expertise and different needs, and this makes the selection of one preferred form of mentoring unwise (Ingleby 2014).

The tensions that exist between competing interpretations of mentoring link to the wider debates that are present in this book about the conflicts that occur across sectors of education in England. Coffield (2004), Lieberman (2009), Lucas (2007), Urban (2009), and Wenger (1998), all draw attention to the different interpretations of the purpose of education that can occur within educational contexts in general. Coffield (2004), Lieberman (2009), and Lucas (2007); develop this theme in particular with respect to FE. These authors are interested in the consequences of education that focuses on what we have seen Urban (2009) refer to as the product of the educational process. Moreover, there is the concern that if too much emphasis is placed on measuring educational products, the attention that is thus given to the educational processes is reduced in importance, a theme that occurs in other chapters of this book, and in the work of Bryan and Carpenter (2008). This chapter therefore reflects on the interplay that exists between these two themes; in other words, the tension that occurs in measuring results and performances yet not fully considering the processes that generate results and performances.

FE MENTORING

Mentoring has appeared as an important pedagogical development within FE in recent years and this section of the chapter outlines how mentoring has become a significant part of the neoliberal FE policy agenda. In 2002 the DfES (The Department for Education and Skills) introduced what was entitled 'Success For All' and the intention of this policy was to reform the English FE sector. In consequence, this change resulted in the formalisation and subsequent development of FE ITT (Initial Teacher Training) mentoring. An important aspect of this process resulted in the establishment of a 'Standards Unit' that was responsible for disseminating best pedagogical practice. In 2002–2003, Ofsted undertook a survey of teacher training and this identified that the taught modules of teacher training programmes were not necessarily linked to the development of practical teaching skills, alongside revealing that mentoring was not as well developed as it could be for FE ITT programmes. This resulted in the DfES Standards Unit introducing a consultation document in 2003b and the subsequent recommendations included the provision of mentors for all trainees and all new lecturers who were working in FE. Both Ofsted and the Standards Unit were in favour of introducing a mentoring system into FE that mirrored the model that was being used within school teacher training. However, Ingleby and Tummons (2012), and Lawy and Tedder (2011, 386) argue that the relatively 'straightforward' nature of the statutory school sector contrasts significantly with the complexity of the FE sector and that it is duplicitous to regard these two educational sectors in the same way. Nonetheless, in another classic example of misguided neoliberal educational policies, this attempt to mirror what happens within the statutory school sector appears to have been accepted in principle throughout the introduction and subsequent development of FE mentoring. Hankey (2004, 390) argues that a further problem with this neoliberal educational policy initiative in FE is that informal mentoring has actually occurred within the sector for years, and this reveals that the neoliberal educational policymakers appear to have not fully understood the full and complex nature of this form of English education. The policy interventions appear to be based on what Lawy and Tedder (2011) outline as being the simplistic assumption that all can be well in FE ITT if the school mentoring system is duplicated, however this fails to take into account the unique complexity of the FE sector.

Hankey (2004, 391) argues that the model of FE ITT mentoring that Ofsted support is based on a hybrid of two of Maynard and Furlong's (1993) models for mentoring. In these mentoring models the ideal mentor is visualised as being an 'expert' and a 'critical friend'. In consequence, a key debate that has emerged within the current FE ITT mentoring system appears to be over the extent to which the mentoring relationship is supporting the professional development of the trainees as opposed to being judgemental about the quality of their teaching. As acknowledged, the subsequent emergence of this model of mentoring is similar to Daloz's (1986) 'support' and 'challenge' approach to mentoring, and this appears to lend itself to judging teaching ability and not necessarily developing reflective practice about the processes of pedagogy. This variability of interpretation of the purpose of mentoring is revealed in the published work of Hankey (2004), Ingleby (2010, 2011), Ingleby and Hunt (2008), Ingleby and Tummons (2012), Lawy and Tedder (2011), and Tedder and Lawy (2009).

Lawy and Tedder (2011) argue that the emergence of 'Success for All' in 2002 within the FE educational sector in England exemplifies an attempt to introduce qualifications that are designed to meet the professional needs of individuals who are working in different educational contexts. This policy initiative appears to have been informed by the Ofsted reports of 2003, 2006, 2007, and 2008. In 2003, Ofsted noted that there was 'a lack of systematic mentoring and support in the workplace' (Ofsted 2003, 2). In 2002, The White Paper, *Further Education: Raising Skills, Improving Life Chances* (2006) led to the introduction of a series of revised standards for FE via LLUK (Lifelong Learning United Kingdom) and these standards were more rigorous and more stringent than the previous FENTO (Further Education National Training Organisation) standards. A form of 'standards-driven' education appears to have become prevalent within FE and this form of pedagogical practice has emerged as an increasingly dominant form of discourse within the FE educational context (Lucas 2007). In consequence, Lawy and Tedder (2011, 386) refer to the introduction of 'a plethora of National Awarding Body qualifications', ranging from 'PTTLS' (Preparing to Teach in the Lifelong Learning Sector) to the 'DTLLS' (Diploma in Teaching in the Lifelong Learning Sector) and it is within this curriculum environment of standards-driven educational initiatives, that mentoring has subsequently developed within FE. Lawy and Tedder (2011, 386) argue that the judgemental nature of Ofsted (as evidenced in the Ofsted report of 2003) has helped to shape the nature of FE mentoring, and that the initial 'ad hoc' nature of FE mentoring 'has been linked formally to college systems and structures including teacher training programmes'.

Alongside the emergence of this interventionist approach to providing mentors for FE trainee teachers and newly qualified educators, there is contention over the definition of mentoring (Hankey 2004; Ingleby and Tummons 2012) as there are what Lawy and Tedder (2011, 389) identify as 'different definitions and models of mentoring' that are available for the professions. The situation is complicated further due to the influence of a complex range of public and private sector organisations in England (for example the NHS [National Health Service]; social services; the TDA [Training and Development Agency]; the EMCC [European Mentoring and Coaching Council]; and the CIPD [Chartered Institute of Personnel and Development]), who all use mentors in different and particular ways. All of these organisations have a commitment to mentoring, however, they have different understandings of the purpose of mentoring and they do not mirror the 'support and challenge' model that is preferred by Ofsted. In exemplifying this point, the CIPD consider there to be three important parts in the mentoring relationship. These component parts are revealed by Alred et al. (1998) and they are based on the exploration of professional concepts; the generation of new understandings of professional practice; and the subsequent development of effective action planning. This particular mentoring process is identified by Lawy and Tedder (2011, 389) as being 'supportive of learning and development and more informal than coaching'. Moreover, this model of mentoring appears to enable individuals to manage their professional development through nurturing professional skills alongside alleviating problematic personal issues. The key component of this mentoring model appears to be based on developing capability as opposed to the judgement and assessment of competence with respect to professional skills. In contrast, since 2003, Ofsted have viewed FE mentoring in increasingly judgemental ways (Tedder and Lawy 2009). This appears to be based on a philosophy that seeks to assess the impact of mentoring on educational performance by measuring performance against academic results, and as revealed in Chap. 3, this is at the centre of the neoliberal policy rationale within the primary and secondary school system in England too. It is, however, the variety of interpretations that occur of the purpose of mentoring that draws attention to the problems within the neoliberal Ofsted FE mentoring agenda (Tedder and Lawy 2009). After all, it appears to be highly unlikely that the 'support' and 'challenge' model of mentoring will be accepted unilaterally by all stakeholders when there are other (more pedagogically appealing) models of mentoring that are potentially available.

THEORETICAL BACKGROUND

In view of the complexity that appears to characterise the nature of FE mentoring, the theoretical background to this chapter is based on a framework that considers how the FE practitioners navigate a variety of sites and types of knowledge and performance, involving potentially radical changes to the presentation of themselves in this aspect of their professional lives.

In understanding the relationship that exists between FE and mentoring it is helpful to consider theories of literacy as social practice and reflect on how this may affect our understanding of what Eraut (2007) terms the epistemology of practice. Literary texts can be regarded as being 'ways of representing the world to others' (Barton 2007, 34, cited in Ingleby 2019). In FE mentoring the 'texts', about mentoring for example, 'Success for All' in 2002; and the Ofsted reports of 2003, 2006, 2007, and 2008; have resulted in 'literary events' that are considered to be 'occasions in everyday life where the written word has a role' (Barton 2007, 35, cited in Ingleby 2019). The FE curriculum is also informed by other documents that shape its general educational context, for example, The White Paper, *Further Education: Raising Skills, Improving Life Chances* that was published by the DfES in 2006. This reveals what Eraut (2000) refers to as the codified knowledge that FE practitioners are expected to grasp, in other words, what FE is primarily concerned with and organised for. Within FE, it is these textually based media that generate understandings of the curriculum. Moreover, as Eraut (2007, 406) argues, professional practice is shaped by cultural knowledge, and this is acquired via curriculum activities that are assimilated and performed by individuals and formalised into 'personal knowledge'.

In attempting to understand FE mentoring under neoliberalism, the work of Goffman (1971, 26) is also helpful, especially in respect of the notion of social interaction as a performance that results in a set of 'dramaturgical problems' in terms of the presentation of the activity to others. This concept that is associated with Goffman (1971) was introduced earlier in the book in Chap. 2, and it is also helpful in making sense of how FE mentoring is understood. A key element in the construction of what constitutes success in FE practice and the potential challenges to this success is based on a pedagogical performance to an audience of FE practitioners; to students; and to those who are assessing pedagogical performance in FE (for example, neoliberal governments and Ofsted). This observed part of the performance is what Goffman refers to as the 'front' and this includes an ability to control the performance environment, alongside the appropriate use of 'props' (1971, 33). In FE mentoring, the key prop appears to be understanding the purpose of this form of pedagogical activity and this is informed by other aspects of Goffman's (1971) front, including the demeanour of those who are working in FE; their professional practice; and their subsequent impact upon this educational sector. In this educational environment there are both educational audiences and props who can combine together to produce potentially unpredictable elements through their interaction. The research that has been completed on FE mentoring that is presented in the following section of the chapter may be visualised as being one of Goffman's 'back regions' where 'suppressed facts' are revealed (1971, 114). A strength of Goffman's (1971) approach is that this provides insights that are useful in potentially developing the future practice of FE mentoring.

Mentoring, in theory, enables FE practitioners to develop their skills of pedagogy through liaising with colleagues who are able to suggest ways of developing pedagogical practice. However, part of the complexity of achieving the desired performance of professional practice is the need to combine together disparate sources of authority that are assimilated through quite different forms of educational transmission; on the one hand the codified knowledge of literary texts and, on the other, the cultural knowledge that is acquired during professional practice. From the FE practitioner's perspective, it may appear axiomatic that professional practice depends upon learning the necessary technical knowledge 'behind' the skills to be utilised. This is usually placed within the conventional forms of academic pedagogy and this traditional aspect of the pedagogy in FE, is at the forefront and signals the key priorities of the curriculum. In consequence, FE practitioners move across different 'domains' of learning (Barton 2007; Barton et al. 2000; Gee 1996; cited in Ingleby 2019), that is 'different places in life where people act differently and use language differently' (Barton 2007, 39, cited in Ingleby 2019). The research that is presented in the following section of the chapter reveals the challenges that the FE practitioners face in blending together the learning from these different domains of FE into a coherent way of presenting themselves as competent practitioners who are influenced by Ofsted and the educational priorities that are stipulated for FE.

If we apply theories of literacy as social practice to FE mentoring, it appears that the formal literary texts about mentoring are based on a number of different models of mentoring, and that the support and challenge model that Ofsted appear to favour is only one of these mentoring models. This appears to have resulted in the curriculum event of a mentoring model that is judging the performance of the FE lecturers via its implementation by Ofsted (Ingleby 2010, 2011; Ingleby and Hunt 2008; Ingleby and Tummons 2012; Lawy and Tedder 2011; and Tedder and Lawy 2009). However, in respect of social practices, the FE lecturers appear to prefer mentoring models that are more supportive of developing professional practice and less inclined to be based on judgemental models of pedagogy. These views reveal what Goffman (1971) describes as a back region of suppressed facts and the next section of the chapter presents research findings on the views of FE lecturers about the ideal purpose of mentoring. What Eraut (2000) refers to as the codified knowledge that practitioners are expected to grasp can be disputed via cultural knowledge and this is essentially the subjective practices and views from the FE lecturers about the ideal purpose of FE.

Key Research Findings

The research on FE mentoring in England reveal two key findings:

1. The FE mentoring system that has been introduced into England via Ofsted is judgmental of teaching ability and this is critiqued.
2. A developmental model of mentoring that is not judgemental of teaching ability is the preferred option of the FE practitioners.

1. The FE mentoring system that has been introduced into England via Ofsted is judgmental of teaching ability.

Cunningham (2004) is one of a number of scholars who acknowledges that it is beneficial to have a system of effective mentoring for FE staff in England. The importance of mentoring is revealed by the high level of interest in this aspect of pedagogy that has occurred from various neoliberal government bodies. However, as opposed to simply introducing a mentoring system that is judgemental of the teaching ability of the practitioners, Cunningham (2004, 83) advocates 'an institutional architecture for mentoring activity'. This model of mentoring that is being proposed is not simply judgemental of teaching ability, as it is a form of mentoring that enables basic mentoring activities alongside developing those aspects of mentoring that are based on the consideration of a more strategic and longer term significance, for example, 'developing individual mentors' skills' (Cunningham 2004, 83). Cunningham (2004) argues that it is important to visualise mentoring as a building block for the professional development of staff at all levels, as opposed to regarding the mentoring process as being judgemental of teaching abilities. This design of mentoring is regarded by Cunningham (2004, 95) as being 'an intelligent course of action' that is able to rectify the occurrences where FE Colleges in England are struggling to attract and retain their teaching staff. Cunningham (2004, 95) argues that considering the question 'why do they do it?' ought to be at the centre of the introduction and subsequent development of mentoring and that the answer to this question ought to be: because the FE Colleges provide all of the necessary 'architectural features' to enable an effective pedagogical environment. However, in the mentoring system that has been introduced into FE in England by neoliberal governments, this question is not being considered fully.

Lawy and Tedder (2011) reveal that the policy context has had an important influence on the adoption of a mentoring model for FE practitioners that is based on assessing competence. Moreover, it is argued that the separation of 'formative support' from 'the assessment of competence' is an 'unnecessary dichotomy' (Lawy and Tedder 2011, 365). This act of separation appears to result in the dislocation of coherent teaching practices from one another, and this is representative of the impact that educational policies can have when neoliberal policymakers do not have any actual experience of working in the areas that they are making policies about. Lawy and Tedder (2011) make reference to the sense of confusion and uncertainty that is associated with FE mentoring and in particular the problems that have resulted from separating formative and performative models of mentoring. It is argued that the resulting tension is evident in what manifests itself as 'a continuous struggle as managers and mentors find the boundaries of their responsibilities' (Lawy and Tedder 2011, 393). The confusion appears to result from the tensions that are present in the interpretations of the role as being either akin to a subject coach, or as someone who is operating as an assessor of meeting particular criteria

(Lawy and Tedder 2011). In consequence, the tension that results from this judgemental model of mentoring is between a 'dyadic' model of mentoring (with the mentor and mentee) and a 'triadic' from of mentoring that brings a third party of 'assessor' into the mentoring relationship (Lawy and Tedder 2011, 393).

The tensions that Lawy and Tedder (2011) reflect on are also evident in the research that has been completed on FE mentoring by Garbutt et al. (2013). It is once again, the policy landscape that appears to be producing the tensions that are made apparent in judging the teaching abilities of FE practitioners. Garbutt et al. (2013, 239) refer to the experience of 'a cultural collision' that is occurring between the FE practitioners and the marketized cultures in which they are operating, as neoliberal policymakers intervene within FE in England in order to make educational practices happen. Garbutt et al. (2013, reveal the complexities that are associated with mentoring as a form of pedagogy in general, and moreover the authors reveal that these problems are exacerbated in the Literacy curriculum. In their research, Garbutt et al. (2013, 253) reveal that a key finding from their work is the 'strength of the developmental culture of Literacy mentors'. This pedagogical aspect of the role of Literacy tutors appears to be at odds with the concept of mentors 'observing' in ways that are similar to the practice of Ofsted inspectors. Moreover, the summative grade that is provided following observation is a form of contrary practice compared to the development of the 'pedagogical values' that are central to the field of Literacy education (Garbutt et al. 2013, 254). It appears that the process of grading and judging teaching does not fit readily into the cultural values that are shared across this particular subject in FE in England and that this is a consequence of what is referred to as being 'a policy maelstrom' (Garbutt et al. 2013, 254).

Tummons and Ingleby (2012) also reflect on the pedagogical consequences of a mentoring model that is judgemental of the abilities of the mentees. Once more, the theme of the complexity of mentoring in FE is apparent in the research of Tummons and Ingleby (2012) with three key themes emerging in their research. Mentors and mentees appear to have complex and at times contradictory interpretations of the purpose of their respective roles; their professional relationships; and the formality or otherwise of these relationships. This one research case study reveals that mentoring in FE is complex and particular and that it is hard to generalise an area of pedagogy that is characterised by such complexity. Within the research, Tummons and Ingleby (2012) make reference to the problems that are apparent in implementing a mentoring system that is judgemental of the practitioners' teaching abilities. FE mentoring is characterised by 'variability' and by 'a lack of systematic guidance' (Tummons and Ingleby 2012, 38). 'Gaps' are apparent in the pedagogical intersubjectivity that exists between mentors and mentees and the relationships that unfold are 'complex and variable'. It is also apparent that any examples of positive relationships occurring between mentors and mentees appear to be based on 'good fortune' as opposed to being the product of a systematic system of mentoring (Tummons and Ingleby, 38). It is recommended that the 'systematic foundations' that will result in a positive system of mentoring need to be developed through a coherent pedagogical philosophy as opposed to being based simply on a will to judge the pedagogical performance of the mentees (Ingleby and Tummons 2012, 38).

2. A developmental model of mentoring that is not judgemental of teaching ability is the preferred option of the FE practitioners.

Cunningham (2004) reflects on the ways in which the mentoring model that has been adopted for FE educators has been forced upon the sector by Ofsted. In Cunningham's (2004, 278) research, it is acknowledged that the formal recognition of the importance of mentoring in teaching is a relatively recent development and that in the late 1980s there was not 'a single index entry against mentors'. However, it gradually became apparent that those educators who were being supported and developed by mentors became more committed to teaching, and this reveals the importance of nurturing a developmental model of mentoring in FE. For Cunningham (2004, 279) what is essential, if mentoring is to develop effectively, is the consideration of the 'ways in which professionalism in mentoring' can be 'incentivised, enhanced and disseminated'. What appears to be crucial in nurturing the FE workforce effectively is to ensure that there is a form of mentoring that is developmental in nature. In order to enable an effective mentoring model, Cunningham (2004) makes a number of recommendations that include: nurturing mentor training; embedding mentoring within organisational culture; and providing financial incentives for mentoring. Cunningham's (2004) research reveals that mentoring is important if pedagogy in FE is to be effective, however there ought to be more than just focusing on mentoring as a means of judging teaching ability if this is to become a helpful aspect of FE professionalism.

Cullimore (2006) refers to the importance of ensuring that there is evidence of joined-up training if mentoring in FE is to move beyond judging the teaching ability of the educators. Cullimore (2006, 303) acknowledges that one of the challenges in developing mentoring effectively rests in addressing the 'debate, consultation and change in this area' of education because the consequences of this turbulent educational landscape evidence 'struggles for identity, proper recognition and satisfactory regulation'. If a developmental model of FE mentoring is to occur, Cullimore (2006) emphasises the importance of providing training for mentors that is effective. The nature of the format and the content that is discussed in mentor meetings is also considered to be in need of being nurtured, however Cullimore (2006, 315) argues that the effective implementation of these recommendations is particularly challenging 'when the goalposts are changing all the time' and when there are 'inconsistencies in the quality of mentoring which the trainees receive'. Although there appears to be a consensus in general from the educators that they would like to have a model of mentoring in FE that is developmental, putting this consensus into effect appears to be particularly challenging. This is because of the complicated nature of the sector for as Cullimore (2006) argues, the FE sector is shaped by a number of complex educational and political organisations including the government; University education departments who are training FE educators; and Colleges. These complex organisations can have 'very different notions of joined-up training' and this can work against the successful development of FE mentoring (Cullimore 2006, 315).

Manning and Hobson (2017) reflect on the ambiguity that appears to exist between judgemental and developmental models of mentoring. Manning and Hobson (2017) complement the previous research that was completed by Tummons and Ingleby (2012) as they argue that there are examples of variable practice in FE mentoring. It is revealed that whereas the mentors consider that their role in FE mentoring is 'developmental', in contrast, the mentees are experiencing a relationship that is regarded as being 'judgemental' (Manning and Hobson 2017, 574). It appears that there are varying perceptions of the impact of mentoring between mentors and mentees and as Manning and Hobson (2017, 589–590) note, 'even if mentors report their approach as developmental, mentees may perceive the same mentoring interaction as being judgemental'. Although the ideal role of the mentoring relationship may be perceived as being developmental, it appears that the mentors are adopting a form of mentoring that becomes judgemental (Manning and Hobson 2017). This highlights the importance of ensuring that 'there is the implementation of a robust system of education for FE mentors, so that the understanding, awareness and skills to adopt a more multifaceted, developmental approach' can be enabled (Manning and Hobson 2017, 590). Moreover, Manning and Hobson (2017) argue that the judgemental model of mentoring actually inhibits the progress of the mentees as the mentoring experience is regarded as being negative, whereas in contrast developmental mentoring results in 'active learning taking place' so that the mentor mentee relationship becomes 'potentially more memorable'. The research findings of Manning and Hobson (2017, 591) are highly relevant for neoliberal policymakers in education because one of the key recommendations from the research evidence base is that:

> Ofsted should remove the requirement for mentors to assess teacher students and instead advocate a developmental mentoring approach whereby mentors encourage mentees to manage their ongoing learning and realise their professional autonomy

The potential that mentoring holds for effective professional development is revealed by Swap et al. (2001). In their research, Swap et al. (2001) argue that the effective development of individuals in educational contexts is enabled by managers who are able to recognise how individuals teach and learn informally at individual levels. The complexity of organisations is again a key theme that is acknowledged by Swap et al. (2001) so the research is especially relevant to the FE sector. It is argued that 'skills, managerial systems, and norms and values, woven into interdependent systems of knowledge termed core capabilities, are critical to any organization' (Swap et al. 2001, 108), and that if there is a system of developmental mentoring in place, this can help enormously in the effective nurturing of the professional organisation. The FE sector has been referred to previously via the Hayes (2007) descriptor as a Cinderella sector of education. It appears that within mentoring there is a possibility to develop what is seen as a 'poor relation' into a functioning and working form of education that can be of benefit to individuals. Swap et al. (2001) argue that an advantage of having mentors is revealed upon considering that lots of mentors have been involved in teaching and learning for many years. However, a key theme of their research is that 'mentoring takes time and continuity' (Swap et al. 2001, 108). As opposed to simply accepting the need for a mentoring model that judges the ability of the FE educators to teach, it appears that a more refined model of mentoring is needed, and this is one that ought to place the developmental needs of those working in FE at the centre of its pedagogical philosophy.

CONCLUDING DISCUSSION

Minott (2010) and Tigelaar et al. (2005) argue that teaching can only develop effectively when we reflect on existing knowledge, beliefs and experiences by considering how teaching processes are being informed. In developing this argument, Minott (2010, 327) emphasises the importance of 'understanding of what works' within teaching and learning so that these experiences can be used to enhance future student learning. This in turn appears to encourage the development of innovative pedagogy that enables academics and learners to develop the curriculum for academic purposes in entirety (Tummons 2011). Minott (2010) also argues that reflective processes are more likely to occur upon considering the prevailing work ethos so that developmental actions can in turn be enabled. This chapter has highlighted the judgemental model of mentoring that has been introduced into FE by the neoliberal quango Ofsted. The literature in the previous section reveals that shared understandings of mentoring ought to be used to develop this aspect of pedagogy in FE, so that professional identity is neither isolated nor becomes overly subjective (Coldron and Smith 1999). However, the influence of neoliberalism produces a form of mentoring heterotopia within a socially and culturally constructed sector of education.

Lawy and Tedder (2011) argue that the performative model of mentoring has been imposed on FE via successive neoliberal governments through Ofsted. This model of mentoring is based on the idea that ineffective teaching can be improved through assessing the performance of mentees to ensure world class standards (Ingleby 2014). The consequence, as acknowledged in the previous section of the chapter is also commented on by Colley (2003) who refers to a triadic relationship in which the dyadic relationship between the mentor and the mentee is shaped by a neoliberal third party (Ofsted). In fact, as argued by Lawy and Tedder (2011, 393), there is no 'best practice' model for mentoring. This is revealed upon acknowledging that the 'support' and 'judge' model of mentoring does little to facilitate the personal, social, and general pedagogical development of the FE educators. In another occurrence of a neoliberal intervention in education in the UK, we see a further example of what Coffield (2006) refers to as 'running ever faster down the wrong road'. To rectify this situation, Coffield (2006) calls for a return to the Platonic notion of 'philosopher kings' who make policies based on expertise as opposed to neoliberal policymakers who have no professional experience of being educators. Ingleby and Hunt (2008), Ingleby (2010, 2011), Ingleby and Tummons (2012), Lawy and Tedder (2011), and Tedder and Lawy (2009) all support a FE mentoring system that nurtures reflective practice. It is argued that this will in turn lead to the emergence of a form of mentoring that facilitates self-directed professional development (Ingleby 2014).

Randall and Downie (1996) and Ingleby and Tummons (2012) argue for the importance of reflecting on the real purpose of education. Is the purpose of mentoring in FE really to judge the ability of the educators to teach? If this is not the case and if a broader model of FE mentoring can be established, this holds the potential for the educational processes and products of FE mentoring to be unified, and this in turn may become a way in which the mentoring relationship can be developed in the future. The stability of having an educational philosophy informing the development of FE mentoring may then in turn result in what Lawy and Tedder (2011, 394) refer to as 'an opportunity for reflection and consolidation'. However, if this sense of stability is to occur, the 'support' and 'judge' model of FE mentoring requires the radical overhaul that is acknowledged by Ingleby (2014).

In this chapter we have reflected on FE mentoring by applying Goffman's concept of 'dramaturgical problems' (1971, 26) and this reveals that FE mentoring occurs in different 'domains' of learning (Barton 2007; Barton et al. 2000; Gee 1996, cited in Ingleby 2019) 'where people act differently and use language differently' (Barton (2007, 39, cited in Ingleby 2019). This results in FE mentors and mentees becoming immersed in different types of learning (Eraut 2000, 2007) and it is revealed that this can pose particular problems when these forms of learning are seen as contradicting each other. It has been argued that mentoring as a form of pedagogy for FE holds the potential to bridge competing domains of pedagogy, and that ideally the FE educators are provided with insights into the personal knowledge that is necessary for successful pedagogical practice. However, as the chapter reveals, there are challenges to the blending together of the knowledge, events and performances that are associated with FE mentoring due to the prevailing influence of neoliberal governments.

REFERENCES

Alred, G., B. Garvey, and R. Smith. 1998. *Mentoring pocketbook*. Alresford: Management Pocketbooks.

Anderson, E.M., and A. Shannon. 1988. Towards a conceptualisation of mentoring. *Journal of Teacher Education* 39 (1): 38–42.

Barton, D. 2007. *Literacy: An introduction to the ecology of written language*. Oxford: Blackwell Publishing.

Barton, D., M. Hamilton, and R. Ivanić. 2000. *Situated literacies: Reading and writing in context*. London: Routledge.

Bryan, H., and C. Carpenter. 2008. Mentoring: A practice developed in community. *Journal of In-service Education* 34 (1): 47–59.

Coffield, F. 2004. *Learning styles and pedagogy in post-16 learning; a systematic and critical review*. London: The Learning and Skills Research Centre.

———. 2006. *Running ever faster down the wrong road*, Inaugural Lecture. London: London University Institute of Education.

Coldron, J., and R. Smith. 1999. Active location in teachers' construction of their professional identities. *Journal of Curriculum Studies* 31 (4): 711–726.

Colley, H. 2003. *Mentoring for social inclusion: A critical approach to nurturing mentor relationships*. London: Routledge.

Cullimore, S. 2006. Joined-up training: Improving the partnership links between a university PGCE (FE) course and its placement colleges. *Research in Post-compulsory Education* 11 (3): 303–317.

Cunningham, B. 2004. Some have mentoring thrust upon them: The element of choice in mentoring in a PCET environment. *Research in Post-compulsory Education* 9 (2): 271–282.

Daloz, J. 1986. *Effective mentoring and teaching*. San Francisco: Jossey Bass.

Eraut, M. 2000. Non-formal learning and tacit knowledge in professional work. *British Journal of Educational Psychology* 70 (1): 113–136.

———. 2007. Learning from other people in the workplace. *Oxford Review of Education* 33 (4): 403–422.

Garbutt, G., D. Orrock, and R. Smith. 2013. Culture clash: Mentoring student literacy educators in a marketised and instrumentalist further education policyscape. *Research in Post-compulsory Education* 18 (3): 239–256.

Gee, J.P. 1996. *Social linguistics and literacies*. London: Routledge Falmer.

Goffman, E. 1971. *The presentation of the self in everyday life*. London: Pelican Books.

Hankey, J. 2004. The good, the bad and other considerations: Reflections on mentoring trainee teachers in post-compulsory education. *Research in Post-compulsory Education* 9 (3): 389–400.

Hayes, D. 2007. *A lecturer's guide to further education: Inside the 'cinderella sector*. Milton Keynes: Open University Press.

Ingleby, E. 2010. Robbing Peter to pay Paul: The price of standards-driven education. *Research in Post-compulsory Education* 15 (1): 427–441.

———. 2011. Asclepius or Hippocrates? Differing interpretations of post-compulsory initial teacher training mentoring. *Journal of Vocational Education & Training* 63 (1): 15–25.

———. 2014. Developing reflective practice or judging teaching performance? The implications for mentor training. *Research in post-compulsory education* 19 (1): 18–33.

———. 2019. It does more than it says on the tin! Problematising higher education in further education in England. *Studies in Higher Education* 44 (1–2): 20–31.

Ingleby, E., and J. Hunt. 2008. The CPD needs of mentors in post-compulsory initial teacher training in England. *Journal of In-service Education* 34 (1): 61–74.

Ingleby, E., and J.E. Tummons. 2012. Repositioning professionalism: Teachers, mentors, policy and praxis. *Research in Post-compulsory Education* 17 (2): 163–179.

Kennedy, A. 2005. Models of CPD: A framework for analysis. *Journal of In-service Education* 31 (2): 235–250.

Lawy, R., and M. Tedder. 2011. Mentoring and individual learning plans: Issues of practice in a period of transition. *Research in Post-compulsory Education* 16 (3): 385–396.

Lieberman, J. 2009. Reinventing teacher professional norms and identities: The role of lesson study and learning communities. *Professional Development in Education* 35 (1): 83–99.

Lucas, N. 2007. Rethinking initial teacher education for further education teachers: From a standards-led to a knowledge-based approach. *Teaching Education* 18 (2): 93–106.

Manning, T., and A. Hobson. 2017. Judgemental and developmental mentoring in further education initial teacher education in England: Mentor and mentee perspectives. *Research in Post-compulsory Education* 22 (4): 574–595.

Maynard, T., and J. Furlong. 1993. Learning to teach and models of mentoring. In *Echoes from Freire for a critically engaged pedagogy*, ed. P. Mayo. London: Bloomsbury. 2013.

Minott, M.A. 2010. Reflective teaching as self-directed professional development: Building practical or work-related knowledge. *Professional Development in Education* 36 (2): 325–338.

Ofsted (Office for Standards in Education). 2003. *The initial training of further education teachers in England: A survey*. London: HMSO.

———. 2006. *The initial training of further education teachers: Findings from 2004/05 inspection of courses leading to national awarding body qualifications*. London: Ofsted.

———. 2007. *The initial training of further education teachers*. London: Ofsted.

———. 2008. *The initial training of further education teachers.* London: Ofsted.

Randall, F., and R.S. Downie. 1996. *Palliative care ethics: A good companion (Oxford Medical Publications).* Oxford: Oxford University Press.

Swap, W., D. Leonard, M. Shields, and L. Abrams. 2001. Using mentoring and storytelling to transfer knowledge in the workplace. *Journal of Management Information Systems* 18 (1): 95–114.

Tedder, M., and R. Lawy. 2009. The pursuit of 'excellence': Mentoring in further education initial teacher training in England. *Journal of Vocational Education and Training* 61 (4): 413–429.

Tigelaar, D., D. Dolmanns, W. Grave, I. Wolfhangen, and C. Vleuten. 2005. Participants' opinions on the usefulness of a teaching portfolio. *Medical Education* 40 (4): 371–378.

Tummons, J.E. 2011. It sort of feels uncomfortable: Problematising the assessment of reflective practice. *Studies in Higher Education* 36 (4): 471–483.

Tummons, J.E., and E. Ingleby. 2012. The problematics of mentoring, and the professional learning of trainee teachers in the English further education sector. *International Journal of Adult Vocational Education and Technology* 3 (1): 29–40.

Urban, M. 2009. Strategies for change: rethinking professional development to meet the challenges of diversity in the early years profession. Paper presented at the IPDA conference, 27–28 November, Birmingham, UK.

Wenger, E. 1998. *Communities of practice: Learning, meaning and identity.* Cambridge: Cambridge University Press.

CHAPTER 6

Neoliberalism and Higher Education

INTRODUCTION

This chapter considers the influence of neoliberalism on HE in FE in England. The research content of the chapter reflects on the nature of this form of higher education in England by considering that the neoliberal policymakers in England ideally wish to see higher education leading to vocational expertise and employability. The chapter explores whether or not the perceptions of the neoliberal policymakers are shared by the academics and students who work and study in HE in FE. The chapter reveals that although some of the academics and students reflect some of the views of the neoliberal policymakers, other interpretations of HE in FE are present that differ from the policy documents. Once more, the chapter interprets this educational context according to a theoretical framework that is based on interpreting theories of literacy as social practice. This enables the chapter to make an original contribution in knowledge to an under-researched form of higher education in England. The neoliberal policy documents that are shaping HE in FE (for example The Browne Report), refer to a sector of education and this oversimplifies this higher education context. In fact, a complex mix of students and institutions are present within HE in FE and the neoliberal policymakers do not appear to take into consideration the rich and varied variables that make up HE in FE. 'Employability' and 'skills' are frequent words that are found within

© The Author(s), under exclusive license to Springer Nature Switzerland AG 2021
E. Ingleby, *Neoliberalism Across Education*, Palgrave Studies on Global Policy and Critical Futures in Education,
https://doi.org/10.1007/978-3-030-73962-1_6

the policy documents, however the academic tutors and the students who are working and studying in HE in FE do not necessarily interpret the sector in this way. Once again, this reveals the tension in policy and practice that has been made evident throughout the chapters of this book.

This chapter content essentially explores the context of HE in FE in England and this reveals the divergent views that are present about its philosophical purpose. If we consider the Latin origins of the word 'education', we may see the purpose of education as enabling individuals to move beyond their current understanding of the world, so that existence is considered in new and alternative ways. However, as the book's chapters have revealed, there are other understandings of the purpose of education, and this is exemplified by the changing nature of higher education in England in recent years, and the ways whereby the students are portrayed as consumers of educational products. In The Browne Report (2010) it is acknowledged that: 'students will direct where money goes through their choice of course and institution' (2010, 27). This perception of the students as consumers of higher education has emerged to become a noteworthy element of the discourse about higher education in England. There are also other understandings of the purpose of higher education and one of these interpretations that links directly to this chapter is the portrayal of HE in FE as a vocational form of higher education (DfES 2003; BIS 2009; Parry 2003, 2007; Ingleby 2019). In developing this theme of the variability of interpretations of the purpose of HE, the chapter presents research findings from literature to explore the views of academics and students about the purpose of HE in England. The research considers whether or not the academic tutors and the students agree with the neoliberal policymaker interpretations of the purpose of higher education in England that are present within three key policy documents (DfES 2003; BIS 2009; and The Browne Report 2010). Abbas et al. (2012) argue that these policy documents have essentially shaped the current higher education context in England in general. At this point in the chapter, it is important to qualify that not all of the policymakers who are operating in this neoliberal context are united in their views on the purpose of higher education. Moreover, although the three policy documents (DfES 2003; BIS 2009; and The Browne Report 2010) have similar themes, there are significant differences of focus and in exemplifying this point, whereas The Browne Report is concerned with the financing of higher education, DfES 2003 and BIS 2009 explore issues of access, equity and employability in respect of higher education. These three policy documents are important because they reveal the key neoliberal New Labour and Conservative Liberal Democrat Coalition governments' interpretation of the purpose of higher education in England that has been maintained during the subsequent Conservative administrations from 2015. In many ways, the policy documents present the higher education context in overly simple ways (Ingleby 2015) and in DfES (2003) and BIS (2009), the complex history of higher education in England is largely disregarded (Abbas et al. 2012). Importantly, DfES (2003) and BIS (2009), and The Browne Report (2010) are framed within distinct political, economic, and philosophical agendas. In DfES (2003) and BIS (2009), 'Good teaching' is regarded as being a particularly important indicator of the 'high quality' that will lead to 'employability' (Ingleby 2015, 521). The Browne Report (2010, 2) advocates the importance of nurturing 'competition' in the higher education system in order to maximise 'quality'. It becomes apparent, therefore, that the unifying theme within the three policy documents is based on a neoliberal regulation of higher education through market forces (Ingleby 2015). The content of this chapter reveals that the academic tutors, the students and the policymakers have different interpretations of the purpose of HE in FE, as the published academic research about HE in FE show that there are not separate interpretations of the nature of higher education that are exclusive to the policymakers, the academic tutors, and the students. At times, the interpretations are different and yet there are other occasions where the interpretations are similar. In exemplifying this argument, although the policy documents emphasise the importance of 'good teaching' 'in its own right' (Ingleby 2015, 521) this is different to the reflections that are provided by the academic tutors and the students in the published research about this form of pedagogy, as the emphasis is placed on the importance of developing 'reflective practice' through 'good teaching' (Ingleby 2019). Accessing this form of pedagogy is regarded as being especially important and the fundamental basis of the neoliberal policymakers' interpretation of 'good teaching' is disputed in this example. The chapter reveals that this results in a fascinating interplay of discursive interpretations about the purpose of HE in FE. The chapter content also considers the work of van Andel et al. (2012) who apply Foucault's theory of 'power' (1971, 1972, 1977) in considering 'students' as 'consumers' of higher education. In van Andel, Pimentel Botas and Huisman's (2012, 68) work, it is argued that 'power is implicitly part of the consumerism debate'. However, Foucault's work has been critiqued by McNay (1994, 5) as 'a dystopian account of post-Enlightenment events within which there occurs a Nietzschean will to power, oppression, disciplinary regulation and subjugation'. In this chapter there is no consideration of the policy-makers, the academic tutors and the students as if they are in 'a Nietzschean will to power'. Instead, there appear to be wider structural factors that are shaping this educational context, and this is why there is the application of an epistemological interpretation of theories of literacy as social practice to HE in FE in the chapter. The context appears to be informed by text-based literacy artefacts producing 'literary events', in other words, activities 'where literacy has a role' (Tummons 2014, 35) and 'literary practices', that is the 'ways that people use language in all sorts of social contexts' (Tummons 2014, 36).

HE in FE

The research findings that are presented in the chapter come from published research on HE in FE (for example Ingleby 2019; and Parry 2003, 2007). The unification of University and non-University education in England in 1992 led to the subsequent expansion of HE in FE (Young 2006) and by the year 2000, the establishment of the LSC (or Learning and Skills Council) resulted in the separation of higher education delivered in Universities and Colleges from the rest of the post-compulsory education sector (Ingleby 2019; Parry 2003). In consequence there occurred a heightened sense of the importance of vocational higher education as a sector of education in its own right in England. Moreover, HE in FE expanded so quickly that by 2015, approximately 9% of higher education provision in England and Wales was taking place within Colleges of Further Education in England and Wales (Parry et al. 2012; Tummons Orr and Atkins 2013). The pedagogy that occurs in these institutions is influenced by a number of variables and this includes differing financial arrangements with University partners alongside differing structures of management (Ingleby 2019). Some Colleges are quite independent as educational institutions and have degree awarding powers, whereas other Colleges work more closely with their local University partners (Creasy 2013; Ingleby 2019). In May 2015, approximately 175,000 students were studying at not only undergraduate levels but also at postgraduate levels in more than 280 Colleges in England (AOC 2015; Ingleby 2019). Importantly, the academic curriculum in this educational context is influenced significantly by what Abbas et al. (2012) refer to as an employability agenda. Abbas et al. (2012) and Ingleby (2019) argue that the key neoliberal policy documents that have shaped higher education in England (for example DfES 2003; BIS 2009; and The Browne Report 2010) reveal the agenda that is informing the neoliberal interest in higher education policy in England. This employability agenda is acknowledged in BIS (2009, 16) as being: 'Our challenge is to nurture a higher education system responsive to the demands of both undergraduate and postgraduate training, embedded and integrated into a wider education and skills framework'. A second key policy theme informing this agenda is the importance of enabling student choice (Ingleby 2019). 'Students can make well-informed choices based on an understanding of the nature of the teaching programme they can expect and the long-term employment prospects it offers' (BIS 2009, 12).

The English neoliberal policymakers appear to regard HE in FE as a particularly useful form of higher education because of its 'widening participation' agenda (Thomas 2001; Ingleby 2019) and this links to a central theme within BIS 2009 through enabling 'fair access on merit and potential regardless of family background' (BIS 2009, 16). The current research into this sector of education in recent years identifies the complexity of this educational context (Ingleby 2015, 2019; Parry and Thompson 2002; Parry 2003, 2007; Parry et al. 2012). There is variability across teaching, learning, management and administration according to institutions (Ingleby 2019). There are also inconsistencies in respect of accessing HE in FE (Burton et al. 2012), different levels of student retention and achievement (Schofield and Dismore 2010), diverse forms of governance of HE in FE (Harwood and Harwood 2004; Trim 2001), and diverse levels of teaching staff within academic programmes (Burkill et al. 2008; Feather 2010, 2012; Wilson and Wilson 2011). The HE in FE context is complex and as Ingleby (2019) argues, the sector 'does more than it says on the tin'. The English neoliberal policymakers, the academic staff, the students, the management, and the administrative staff exist within a complex form of vocational education that is both 'unique' (Burton et al. 2012, 25) and 'experimental' (Parry 2007). Moreover the 'contestation' within HE in FE appears to generate an educational context that is complex and this in turn holds the potential for the generation of new interpretations of the purpose of higher education (Creasy 2013, 39; Ingleby 2019; Parry 2007).

THEORETICAL BACKGROUND

The work of van Andel et al. (2012, 67) is relevant to this chapter as it explores the neoliberal interest in higher education through the application of a theory of power relations via the argument that 'power is implicitly part of the consumer debate'. Ingleby (2019) notes that this argument develops the work of Delucchi and Korgen (2002) as power is interpreted as being 'neither self-contained nor self-sufficient' (van Andel et al. 2012, 68). The dynamics of power and its 'exchange' are considered to depend on the complexity of human interaction and subsequently this can result in 'resistance' to policies and practices via 'power struggles' (van Andel et al. 2012, 68 cited in Ingleby 2019). This interpretation of power is based on Foucault's argument that 'relations of power are everywhere because freedom is everywhere' (van Andel et al. 2012, 68), because Foucault (1971) argues that during 'discourse' (or, in our conversations about the world) we witness the exercise of power (Hudson 2003, 134, cited in Ingleby 2019). The conversations in society reveal what Foucault (1972, 49) refers to as a 'regime of truths' within social spaces and it can be argued that within HE in FE in England, a 'regime of truths' is constituted from 'texts' (policy documents, curriculum documents, academic books and articles), curriculum 'events' (activities generated from these documents) and stakeholder 'practices'- individual interpretations of these curriculum events (Ingleby 2019). In order to develop the research interest that is already present in HE in FE, this chapter presents an epistemological discussion that is based on interpreting theories of literacy as social practices within this research context.

In complementing the work of van Andel et al. (2012), and Ingleby (2019), the chapter content reveals the differing interpretations of the purpose of higher education that are present within the academics and students who work and study in this research context. These varying interpretations appear to be based on a combination of subjective and objective factors. Ingleby (2019) argues that the policy documents that are shaping the educational context (DfES 2003; BIS 2009; The Browne Report 2010) can be regarded as being examples of 'literary texts' (Barton 2007; Barton et al. 2000; Gee 1996). However, as opposed to exploring the 'power relations' of this context and considering the presence or otherwise of a 'will to power' (McNay 1994; van Andel et al. 2012) within this educational context, the chapter focuses on the literary texts, events and practices that are shaping HE in FE. As Ingleby (2019) argues, McNay's

(1994) critique of Foucault's emphasis on a dystopian 'will to power' in individuals can be addressed by regarding the HE in FE context as form of literacy as social practice.

In the previous chapter, literacy was defined by using Barton's (2007, 34) work and summarised as being a 'symbolic system used for communication'. In consequence, literary texts are 'ways of representing the world to others' (Barton 2007, 34, cited in Ingleby 2019). Texts (like DfES 2003; BIS 2009; and The Browne Report 2010) become the basis of 'literary events' that are understood as being 'occasions in everyday life where the written word has a role' (Barton 2007, 35, cited in Ingleby 2019). The academic degrees within HE in FE each have an individual curriculum that is informed by the policy documents that shape its wider educational context. Other texts (for example the QAA [Qualification Assurance Agency] benchmark statements for foundation degrees [2010]), alongside subject specialist books also inform the curriculum events that are enabled by the academic tutors within this context. These curriculum events are informed by 'literary practices' that are defined as being distinctive ways of 'using reading and writing in particular situations' (Barton 2007, 36, cited in Ingleby 2019). Scribner and Cole (1981, 234–238) reveal that literary practices are ways of using literacy from one particular situation to another related situation (Ingleby 2019). This epistemological understanding of literacies as social practice has been applied to the chapter in order to explore the discourse of the policymakers, the academic tutors and the students in their respective 'domains' (Barton 2007; Barton et al. 2000; Gee 1996, cited in Ingleby 2019). 'Domains' are defined by Barton (2007, 39) as 'different places in life where people act differently and use language differently' and the research in the chapter considers the blending together (or otherwise) of the literary texts, events and practices that are associated with the educational context of HE in FE in England.

KEY RESEARCH FINDINGS

The research findings on HE in FE in England reveal two key themes:

1. HE in FE in England is situated within a broader higher education context that focuses on the importance of regulating the sector by market forces and emphasising the importance of employability.
2. The complexity of HE in FE reveals a diverse sector of higher education that is not served well by overly generalised neoliberal policies.

1. HE in FE in England is situated within a broader higher education context that focuses on the importance of regulating the sector by market forces and emphasising the importance of employability.

The work of Barnett (1992) reveals two important dominant and rival conceptualisations about the purpose of higher education, and in particular, two competing views about what makes for a quality experience in employment and study in HE. One of these interpretations of quality in higher education is referred to by Barnett (1992) as being based on the importance of generating a scholarly academic community. In other words, the nature of the character of the interactions that are taking place in higher education emerge to become of vital importance to the understandings of what constitutes a quality HE experience. In contrast, an alternative perception of quality has emerged under neoliberalism in England in which the inputs and outputs and end products become most important in defining quality in HE in FE. Barnett (1992) argues that this view of quality in higher education is based on considerations of performance and that this is captured via performance indicators. Moreover, 'effectiveness' in higher education in England is measured in respect of meeting neoliberal governments' targets of efficiency (Barnett 1992). Employability and developing vocational skills have emerged to become a key part of the rationale behind the purpose of HE in FE in this latter definition. Barnett (1992) reveals that this interpretation of the purpose of higher education has resulted in the emergence of discursive terms including 'performance indicators'; 'fitness for purpose'; 'value added'; 'peer review'; 'total quality management'; and 'academic audit'. These discursive terms face both externally and internally to higher education in England and they are a key aspect of HE in FE in particular (Ingleby 2019). As well as providing external data that neoliberal governments can use in order to assess particular interpretations of the effectiveness of HE in FE, these discursive terms are used to inform those who are working and studying in the sector about the merits or otherwise of HEIs (Higher Education Institutions) and their academic programmes. Barnett (1992) reflects on the interpretations that have emerged in respect of improving the quality of higher education processes and the nature of the student experience; the skills that are developed in the curriculum; and the processes of higher education institutional quality audit.

Barnett (2011, 39) acknowledges that although the marketised University 'polarises opinion', there are those 'who consider that the contemporary university is placed in a competitive marketplace'. The argument runs that most HEIs in England are funded by the state and that this money is not guaranteed. It is argued by Barnett (2011) that an awareness of marketisation enables HEIs to generate income from sources beyond the state. Moreover, this awareness of a market becomes instrumental to HEIs providing a service for others that is based on 'efficiency' and 'freedom' (Barnett 1992, 39). Barnett (2011) argues that those who consider that the application of market forces to HEIs is akin to defending what is indefensible ought to realise that HEIs experience worldwide market forces because most HEIs have the capacity to generate income from markets. For Barnett (1992, 40) the complexity of HEIs as organisations results in them becoming involved with several markets 'for example knowledge transfer, patents, establishing of private companies' and 'consultancy activities'. It is also argued by Barnett (2011, 41) that HEIs are increasingly offering their services on private levels with the intention of making a financial profit (for example, 'with conference suites and sports and health facilities'). The main operations of HEIs in respect of research and teaching also lend themselves to the discourse of marketisation and this is exemplified with research funding that is often linked to charitable organisations and therefore not the sole preserve of the state. Barnett's (2011) work reveals that the automatic association of HE in FE and state funding is more complex than it may initially appear, and that this is an example of where the rationale for the marketisation of HE in FE is evident. According to Barnett (2011, 59) 'we cannot escape the presence of ideology in higher education and so have to find a way of living effectively with it'. Marketisation appears to be one of these ideologies and just as there are advocates for the principles of marketisation, so there are also those who are opposed to its representation. It appears however, that there are a number of neoliberal policymakers who are in favour of the marketisation of HE, especially in respect of HE in FE, and this theme is developed in the subsequent paragraphs of this section of the chapter.

Ingleby (2015) applies the work of Archer and Leathwood (2003) to reveal that a key component of the neoliberal definition of high quality higher education is based on identifying the type of employment that is gained by students after they have graduated from, HE. As Mayo (2013) reveals, the use of the word 'competences' and its associations with employability, contributes to the dominant discourse that is shaping understandings of HE in England with the implication that there ought to be a clear purpose to HE that can in turn be measured (Ingleby 2015). As we have seen already in this chapter, this association of 'education' with 'employment' occurs as a result of complex neoliberal political and socio-economic processes. As previously noted in Chap. 1, Harris and Islar (2013) and Williams (2013) argue that these neoliberal political and socio-economic processes are based on historical and political discourses where previous and current interpretations of society are used to generate new understandings of the social world (Ingleby 2015). Under the New Labour administrations that were in government in the UK from 1997–2010, this neoliberal conceptualisation of higher education is present in two major white papers that reveal key indicators of government interpretations of the nature of teaching in higher education in England (DfES 2003; BIS 2009). Ingleby (2015) argues that both Blair (2004) and Willetts (2011) claimed that social inequality could be tackled effectively if students from disadvantaged backgrounds are included within the higher education system, and this is especially relevant for HE in FE. Abbas et al. (2012) argue that England has essentially imitated the US and Australia by claiming that the cost of higher education is too expensive for the state. This claim intensified after 2008 due to the economic recession and resulted in a strengthening of the belief that the government was unable to pay the costs of higher education and that market forces were necessary to regulate HE and promote the importance of employability (Slaughter and Rhoades 2004).

Ingleby (2015) argues that neoliberal policy documents like BIS (2009) are typified by making broad and all-encompassing recommendations about higher education in England: 'in encouraging universities to adapt and improve their service' (BIS 2009, 70). This interpretation of higher education reinforces the view that employability and market forces are important. Ingleby (2015) notes that in DfES (2003, 8) 'education' is considered to be 'the best and most reliable route out of poverty and disadvantage'. However, as argued by Ingleby (2019), these general statements about higher education in England do not acknowledge its complexity as a sector of education. In exemplifying this point, Crozier et al. (2008, cited in Ingleby 2015b) argue that the diverse students in higher education are being educated in diverse institutions. A complex profile of institutions and students are present that cannot be explained by all-encompassing statements about the importance of employability and market forces and this argument is particularly relevant to HE in FE. However, the policy documents that are shaping the sector, such as

DfES (2003) and BIS (2009) do not appear to acknowledge this historical complexity within higher education provision in England (Ingleby 2015).

2. The complexity of HE in FE reveals a diverse sector of higher education that is not served well by overly generalised neoliberal policies.

It appears to be too simplistic to consider HE in FE as being restricted to 'market forces' and 'employability' as there is in fact a rich educational context in HE in FE in England that is characterised by many complex aspects (Ingleby 2015). Parry (2003, 308) refers to 'the uncertain and ambiguous role of further education colleges as providers of undergraduate education' in England. Moreover, it is acknowledged by Parry (2003, 308) that the HE in FE sector is particularly complex in respect of 'planning, funding, and quality arrangements' so it is problematic to refer to this form of education by using a few words, for example, 'market forces' and 'employability'. As opposed to considering the HE in FE sector in England in positive ways, Parry (2003, 335) refers to 'the uncertainty and ambiguity' of the sector and its 'awkwardness and unease' and 'uneven and incomplete nature'. Parry (2003, 335) also reveals the changing nature of neoliberal policies in respect of HE in FE in England as what is referred to as a 'zone of low or no policy' becomes one of 'high policy'. There is now an expectation that Colleges, alongside partner HEIs should lead the way in the sector in England, yet this is very different to the traditional perception of the tertiary education sector (Hayes 2007). In another example of neoliberal policymakers in England underestimating the complexity of sectors of education, the blending together of FE and HE appears to be problematic, as it is not possible to refer to a unified sector of education when the two component parts are so very different. There is, it appears, a diverse sector of education that is not being served well by neoliberal policies.

Parry (2007) refers to the scale and pace of the growth of higher education in England under the New Labour administrations from 1997 onwards and argues that the development of HE in FE is a policy experiment. In this policy approach, Colleges and Universities have been encouraged to work together in partnership, yet the complexities that are inherent in differentiation and diversification are challenging (Parry 2007). FE Colleges have become providers of vocational education and training for post-compulsory students alongside catering for the educational needs of 14 year-olds, and in turn offering degree level qualifications, and it is not easy to meet all of the needs of the varied learners who are part of these diverse educational sectors (Parry 2007). Moreover, it appears that any one curriculum area of HE in FE is associated with a variety of complex aspects, including the perceptions of the tutors and the students about their higher education programmes. Ingleby (2019) reveals that not all of the students on HE in FE programmes share the same agendas as the neoliberal policymakers. The students' vision of education appears to be much more complex than merely obtaining a degree and entering the world of employment. Being educated for the sake of being educated emerges as a reason why some of the students in HE in FE want a degree level qualification and this is different to the neoliberal policymaker objectives (Ingleby 2019). The academic tutors who are working in HE in FE also appear to have different perceptions of the purpose of studying for a degree (Ingleby 2015, 2019). 'Developing reflective practice' is one of the key reasons that is cited by the academic tutors in Ingleby's (2019) research for studying in HE in FE, and yet a dominant theme within the policy documents is employment and the recommendation that degrees need to equip graduates with the skills to cope with 'a fast changing work environment' (DfES 2003, 44). Likewise, the neoliberal policymakers recommend ensuring that potential students have the best possible information on the content of courses and on the value in academic and employment terms of specific qualifications (BIS 2009, 12), and yet these reasons for studying in HE in FE are disputed by Ingleby (2015, 2019). Once more it appears that this sector of education is complex and that HE in FE in England is not being developed effectively by neoliberal policymakers.

Parry et al. (2012) reveal that the students who are studying HE in FE come from a diverse range of backgrounds and this strengthens the argument for the importance of understanding the complexity of the sector. Parry et al. (2012, 104) argue that the students who are being educated in HE in FE 'make informed and rational choices about where and what to study'. However, Parry et al. (2012) also reveal that although the students appear to think that they are making informed and rational choices about their form of study, there are disparities, and this works against the idea of there being a market place that is populated with consumers who are making logical choices. Parry et al. (2012, 109) note that most of the disparities with the students are associated with the 'students' modes of study and their qualification awarding body'. More of the students in the research of Parry et al. (2012) thought that they were studying full-time and fewer part-time, when compared to their College's records and this appears to reveal complexities in defining part-time study in HE in FE in England. Alongside the research of Ingleby (2015, 2019), this illustrates a number of the complexities that are present in HE in FE. Parry et al. (2012) also reveal that 12% of the 2,523 students in their research sample were not aware of who their awarding body was. Moreover, of those students who thought that they knew who was awarding their degree, 'fewer thought their qualification was awarded by a university than was the case' (Parry et al. 2012, 109). This complexity in this one example of the students in HE in FE in England reveals that the BIS (2009, 16) recommendation for 'excellent teaching and fair access on merit and potential, regardless of family background' (BIS 2009, 16) is framed within an overly simplistic policy landscape.

Parry and Thompson (2002, 95) argue that the whole area of HE in FE in respect of policy is characterised by 'silences, confusions, and ambiguities'. The work of Parry and Thompson (2002) reveals three key aspects that account for the problems that have been generated in this aspect of neoliberal educational policymaking. These three features are listed by Parry and Thompson (2002, 95) as constituting: 'the slim and disconnected nature of the evidence-base to guide contemporary policy-making; the unstable, uncertain, and unfavourable conditions for colleges to deliver growth; and the asymmetries of power and interest expressed in a dual system of tertiary education'. In view of these challenges and complexities within HE in FE, it is advisable to have policymaking processes that are based on understanding the breadth and depth of HE in FE as opposed to witnessing an emphasis being placed on employability and marketisation.

Concluding Discussion

The research findings that are published about HE in FE reveal an intriguing interplay of discourse that is taking place between the neoliberal policymakers, the academic tutors, and the students. HE in FE is being shaped by a hyper form of capitalism and the neoliberal policymakers have enabled a culture of consumerism within higher education (van Andel et al. 2012; Ingleby 2015, 2019). In the research that is published about HE in FE, the academic tutors and the students reflect on their experiences of this educational sector in rich and varied ways. In interpreting this educational context, van Andel et al. (2012) apply the work of Foucault (1971, 1972, 1977). Ingleby (2019) argues that Foucault does not regard discourse analysis as 'textual analysis' because texts are regarded by Foucault as being 'boundless' and they are not considered to be 'independent discursive units' (Andersen 2003, 9). Moreover, discourse analysis is critiqued by Foucault as a 'pure description of discursive facts' (Foucault 1972, 234, cited in Ingleby 2019) and it is viewed by Foucault as being a 'felicitous positivism' (Andersen 2003, 10). Ingleby (2019) applies the work of van Andel et al. (2012) with its application of Foucault's (1971, 1972, 1977) theory to highlight the power dynamics that operate between consumers of higher education beyond 'texts'. It is argued by Ingleby (2019) that van Andel et al. (2012) are especially interested in power struggles between consumers of higher education and that this work is informed by Burbules (1986), Giddens (1979), and Poulantzas (1978). In complementing the arguments of van Andel et al. (2012), HE in FE in England can be considered via an epistemological interpretation of theories of literacy as social practice (Ingleby 2019). This enables connections to be seen between 'texts', curriculum 'events', and pedagogical 'practices' (Ingleby 2018). The students and the academic tutors are highly influenced by the neoliberal policymakers and their key 'texts' about HE in FE (for example DfES 2003; BIS 2009; and The Browne Report 2010). The pedagogical 'events' that are taking place in HE in FE can also be traced back to these texts (Ingleby 2019). Moreover, the 'practices' (or individual interpretations of these curriculum events) are revealed in the research that has taken place with the academic tutors and the students who are associated with HE in FE. These research participants reveal their personal interpretations of HE in FE and these experiences are influenced by both subjective and objective factors (for example, the subjective wish to be educated and the realisation that HE in FE is associated with market forces [Ingleby 2019]). The whole pedagogical environment of HE in FE appears to be more complex than 'a Nietzschean will to power' (McNay 1994, 5, cited in Ingleby 209), as it is a neoliberal educational context that is being shaped by a number of factors. However, through exploring the texts, events and practices that are associated with HE in FE, it is possible to gain a nuanced understanding of what is happening (Ingleby 2019). The reflections of the research subjects in HE in FE are important because they reveal how subjective practices are informed by the texts that generate curriculum events within this educational sector (Ingleby 2019). If we are to fully comprehend the 'practices' that are occurring, it is important to take into consideration the 'texts' and 'events' that shape this form of higher education. The policy documents, or 'texts' that are influencing HE in FE (for example DfES 2003; BIS 2009; The Browne Report 2010; and The QAA Foundation Degree Benchmark Statements 2010) are informing the curriculum events that are occurring, and this in turn results in the social practices that are revealed in the published research on HE in FE. Ingleby (2019) reveals that the academic tutors who are working in HE in FE emphasise the importance of developing 'reflective practice', and that this is influenced by key texts that are associated with the discipline of early childhood studies (for example the QAA Subject Benchmark Statements for Early Childhood Studies 2014). In this educational policy document, reference is made to the importance of 'reflection on experiences' (2014, 11) and 'reflection on practice' (2014, 13). This is a key theme that is associated with early childhood studies by the academic tutors and the students who are working in this vocational area (Ingleby 2019) and this aspect of professional practice draws on the key texts that are informing this subject area, such as Lindon (2012, 1, cited in Ingleby 2019), where 'all practitioners are expected to reflect on what they do with children and families'. In this example, the professional practice that is being endorsed by the academic tutors who are working on this vocational degree in HE in FE can be traced back to these texts (Ingleby 2019).

The contestation of the concept of students as consumers of educational products that is revealed by Ingleby (2015, 2019), can also be regarded as being an example of 'practice' (or a manifestation of subjective understandings of HE in FE). As Parry et al. (2012) reveal, the students in HE in FE do not necessarily interpret their curriculum events in ways that are the same as the policy texts that have shaped this educational context. In some respects, the work of Parry et al. (2012) reveals that there can be an absence of rational thought in HE in FE as opposed to there being a market place in which consumers are making logical and informed decisions. In this example, the students who are studying in HE in FE are contradicting the statements that are present within the policy documents about HE in FE. After all, obtaining a degree is considered by the neoliberal policymakers as being a key way of realising opportunities (Ingleby 2019).

The next phase of expansion in higher education will hinge on providing opportunities for different types of people to study in a wider range of ways than in the past (BIS 2009, 4). Universities and Colleges play a vital role in expanding opportunity and promoting social justice (DfES 2003, 4). Higher

Education provides a major opportunity for creating social mobility. (The Browne Report 2010, 26)

However, these policy texts are not interpreted in universal ways and the research findings of Ingleby (2019) and Parry et al. (2012) reveal that the presence of 'opportunity' is not necessarily acknowledged by the students who are studying in HE in FE, due to their subjective interpretations of what is happening to them. The chapter reinforces Ingleby's (2019) argument that HE in FE does more than it says on the tin and that many complex dynamics are set in motion via neoliberal social policies (Bagley and Ackerley 2006). In the chapter, we have seen that although the neoliberal educational context of HE in FE is characterised by complexity (Creasy 2013), we are able to understand what is happening by applying an epistemological interpretation of theories of literacy as social practice (Barton 2007; Barton et al. 2000; Gee 1996). The 'texts' (for example the policy documents) result in curriculum 'events' that are interpreted in subjective ways as social 'practices' (Ingleby 2019). This epistemological position enables subjective and objective factors to be considered as they in turn shape what has become a fascinating neoliberal educational context.

REFERENCES

Abbas, A., P. Ashwin, and M. McLean. 2012. Neoliberal policy, quality and inequality in undergraduate degrees. In *Organising neoliberalism: Markets, privatisation and injustice*, ed. P. Crawshaw and P. Whitehead, 181–199. London: Anthem Press.

Andersen, N.A. 2003. *Discursive analytical strategies: Understanding Foucault, Koselleck, Laclau, Luhmann*. Bristol: Policy Press.

Archer, L., and C. Leathwood. 2003. Identities and inequalities in higher education. In *Higher education and social class: Issues of exclusion and inclusion*, ed. L. Archer, M. Hutchings, and A. Ross, 176–191. London: Routledge Falmer.

Atkins, L. 2013. From marginal learning to marginal employment? The real impact of learning employability skills. *Power and Education* 5 (1): 28–37.

Bagley, C.A., and C.L. Ackerley. 2006. 'I am much more than just a mum'. Social capital, empowerment and sure start. *Journal of Education Policy* 21 (6): 717–734.

Barnett, R. 1992. *Improving higher education: Total quality care*. Buckingham: SRHE and Open University Press.

————. 2011. The marketised university: Defending the indefensible. In *The marketisation of higher education and the student as consumer*, ed. M. Molesworth, R. Scullion, and E. Nixon, 39–51. Abingdon: Routledge.

Barton, D. 2007. *Literacy: An introduction to the ecology of written language*. Oxford: Blackwell Publishing.

Barton, D., M. Hamilton, and R. Ivanić. 2000. *Situated literacies: Reading and writing in context*. London: Routledge.

Blair, T. 2004. The prime minister's speech to the IPPR think tank and Universities UK joint conference on higher education reform, 14 January in London.

Browne, J. 2010. *Securing a sustainable suture for higher education: An independent review of higher education funding and student finance*. London: UK Government.

Burbules, N.C. 1986. A theory of power in education. *Educational Theory* 36 (2): 95–114.

Burkill, S., S. Rodway-Dyer, and M. Stone. 2008. Lecturing in higher education in further education settings. *Journal of Further and Higher Education* 32 (4): 321–331.

Burton, K., M. Lloyd, and C. Griffiths. 2012. Barriers to learning for mature students studying HE in an FE college. *Journal of Further and Higher Education* 35 (1): 25–36.

Creasy, R. 2013. HE lite: Exploring the problematic position of HE in FECs. *Journal of Further and Higher Education* 37 (1): 38–53.

Crozier, G., D. Reay, J. Clayton, and L. Colliander. 2008. Different strokes for different folks: Diverse students in diverse institutions- experiences of higher education. *Research Papers in Education* 23 (2): 167–177.

Delucchi, M., and K. Korgen. 2002. 'We're the customer, we pay the tuition'. Student consumerism among undergraduate sociology majors. *Teaching Sociology* 30 (1): 100–107.

Department for Business Innovation and Skills. 2009. *Higher ambitions: The future of universities in a knowledge economy*. Norwich: HMSO.

Department for Education and Skills. 2003. *The future of higher education*. Norwich: HMSO.

Feather, D. 2010. A whisper of academic identity: An HE in FE perspective. *Research in Post-compulsory Education* 15 (2): 189–204.

————. 2012. Do lecturers delivering higher education in further education desire to conduct research? *Research in Post-compulsory Education* 17 (3): 335–347.

Foucault, M. 1971. *Madness and civilisation*. London: Routledge.

————. 1972. *The archaeology of knowledge*. New York: Pantheon.

————. 1977. *Discipline and punish*. London: Allen Lane.

Gee, J.P. 1996. *Social linguistics and literacies*. London: Routledge Falmer.

Giddens, A. 1979. *Central problems in social theory*. Berkeley: University of California Press.

Harris, L., and M. Islar. 2013. Neoliberalism nature and changing modalities of environmental governance in contemporary Turkey. In *Global economic crisis and the politics of diversity*, ed. Y. Atasoy, 52–78. London: Palgrave Macmillan.

Harwood, J., and D. Harwood. 2004. Higher education in further education: Delivering higher education in a further education context: A study of five south west colleges. *Journal of Further and Higher Education* 28 (2): 153–164.

Hayes, D. 2007. *A lecturer's guide to further education: Inside the 'cinderella sector*. Milton Keynes: Open University Press.

Hudson, B. 2003. *Understanding justice: An introduction to ideas, perspectives and controversies in modern penal history*. Buckinghamshire: Open University Press.

Ingleby, E. 2015. The house that Jack built: Neoliberalism, teaching in higher education and the moral objections. *Teaching in Higher Education* 20 (5): 507–518.

———. 2018. Early years educators' perceptions of professional development in England: An exploratory study of policy in practice. *Professional Development in Education* 44 (1): 22–32.

———. 2019. It does more than it says on the tin! Problematising higher education in further education in England. *Studies in Higher Education* 44 (1–2): 20–31.

Ingleby, E., B. Wilford, and C. Hedges. 2019. Teaching with technology and higher education: A brave new world? *Practice: Contemporary Issues in Practitioner Education* 1 (1): 73–87.

Mayo, P. 2013. *Echoes from Freire for a critically engaged pedagogy*. London: Bloomsbury.

McNay, L. 1994. *Foucault: A critical introduction*. Cambridge: Polity Press.

Parry, G. 2003. Mass higher education and the English: Where in the colleges? *Higher Education Quarterly* 57 (4): 308–337.

———. 2007. The English experiment. *Journal of University Studies* 35 (1): 95–110.

Parry, G., and A. Thompson. 2002. *Closer by degrees: The past, present and future of higher education in further education colleges*. London: Learning and Skills Development Agency.

Parry, G., C. Callender, P. Scott, and P. Temple. 2012. *Understanding higher education in further education colleges*. London: Department for Business Innovation and Skills, HMSO.

Poulantzas, N. 1978. *State, power, socialism*. London: New Left Books.

Quality Assurance Authority. 2010. *Foundation degree qualification benchmark*. Gloucester: Quality Assurance Agency for Higher Education.

———. 2014. *Subject benchmark statement: Early childhood studies*. Gloucester: Quality Assurance Agency for Higher Education.

Schofield, C., and H. Dismore. 2010. Predictors of retention and achievement of higher education students within a further education context. *Journal of Further and Higher Education* 34 (2): 207–221.

Scribner, S., and M. Cole. 1981. *The psychology of literacy.* Cambridge, MA: Harvard University Press.

Slaughter, S., and G. Rhodes. 2004. *Academic capitalism and the new economy: Markets states and higher education.* Baltimore, MD: The Johns Hopkins University Press.

Thomas, L. 2001. Power, assumptions and prescriptions: A critique of widening participation policy-making. *Higher Education Policy* 14 (4): 361–377.

Trim, P. 2001. A review of educational partnership arrangements in further and higher education: Pointers for managers in further education. *Research in Post-compulsory Education* 6 (2): 187–203.

Tummons, J.E. 2014. The textual representation of professionalism: Problematising professional standards for teachers in the UK lifelong learning sector. *Research in Post-compulsory Education* 19 (1): 33–44.

Van Andel, J., C. Pimentel Botas, and J. Huisman. 2012. The consumption values and empowerment of the student as customer: Taking a rational look inside higher education's 'Pandora's box'. *Higher Education Review* 45 (1): 62–85.

Willetts, D. 2011. Ron Dearing lecture: universities and social mobility, 17th February, in University of Nottingham, Nottingham.

Williams, J. 2013. *Consuming higher education: Why learning can't be bought.* London: Bloomsbury.

Wilson, A., and B. Wilson. 2011. Pedagogy of the repressed: Research and professionality within HE in FE. *Research in Post-compulsory Education* 16 (4): 465–478.

Young, M. 2006. Further and higher education: Seamless or differentiated future? *Journal of Further and Higher Education* 30 (1): 1–10.

CHAPTER 7

Neoliberalism and Professional Development in Education

Introduction

This chapter explores the perceptions of professional development that are held by selected educators in England. It is argued that there are few examples of what Kennedy (2005) refers to as 'transformative professional development' due to the emphasis that is placed on achieving successful examination results. The chapter content is developed via a theoretical background of literacy as social practice. The 'texts' informing professional development (neoliberal policy documents and their recommendations) result in CPD 'events' and 'activities'. The chapter explores the personal subjective experiences (or 'practices') of CPD that are experienced by selected educators and the content considers the implications that this has for professional development in education in neoliberal contexts. It is argued that the disconnect that exists between policy and practice in neoliberal education produces negative consequences for CPD. As we have seen already in this book, there are many examples of decisions that are being made about education in England that are not based on pedagogical philosophy. The neoliberal policymakers who are making decisions about professional development in education are also not necessarily basing these decisions on professional pedagogical experiences. This book has revealed that there is an education system in England that is not being directed by experienced teachers as the political figures who shape

© The Author(s), under exclusive license to Springer Nature Switzerland AG 2021
E. Ingleby, *Neoliberalism Across Education*, Palgrave Studies on Global Policy and Critical Futures in Education,
https://doi.org/10.1007/978-3-030-73962-1_7

111

education in England are rarely professional educators. Professional development in education in England is therefore not based on pedagogical philosophy. The holistic needs of the educators are in consequence not being met in general and the transformative sense of professional development that Kennedy (2005) recommends is not being realized.

The chapter reflects on the perceptions of selected educationalists about their experiences of professional development that are present in academic research in education. The educators who feature in the research findings section of the chapter have worked in a variety educational settings, including in early years education in England. The first main chapter of this book focused on the application of technology to education in the early years and this final main chapter explores the professional development experiences of those who are educating in the early years. In part, this is to highlight that individual sectors of education like the early years are complex forms of education in themselves and yet the neoliberal policymakers in England frequently refer to these educational contexts in entirety without considering their full complexity. In exemplifying this point, although Waters and Payler (2015, 159) define 'early years educators' as being those 'who are charged, as part of their professional role, with the care and education of young children', the agreed age range of 'early years' varies across countries. This variation appears to depend upon 'curricula, nature of provision and funding arrangements', with 'early years' referring to children who are aged between 'birth to five', 'birth to six or seven', or 'three to seven' (Waters and Payler 2015, 161). However, in general, the consensus appears to be that 'early years' refers to 'birth to seven' (Waters and Payler 2015, 161), although this one example of complexity in definition in one educational sector indicates the numerous variables that ought to be taken into consideration by the policymakers as they implement directives about CPD in this area. In England, a number of the practitioners in the published research on professional development in education have been influenced by the Every Child Matters agenda that was launched in England in 2003 in an attempt to promote collaboration and partnership between education, health, and care (Waller 2005). Moreover, the professional development of early years educators in England has been influenced by The EYFS (or Early Years Foundation Stage) that emerged as a consequence of The Every Child Matters agenda (Ingleby 2016). Like many other neoliberal policies in England, there appears to be a 'blanket approach' within the EYFS that emphasises the importance of developing children's skills in what The Nutbrown Review (2012) refers to as 'quality learning' in association with 'quality professionals'. The published research on professional development in this area reveals that CPD rarely appears to result in the generation of what is phrased by Kennedy (2005) as the development of a 'community of professional practice'. The work of Urban (2009) refers to the presence of a perception by neoliberal policy-makers that early years educators ought to be 'solvers of problems' and in exploring the presence of this perception, the chapter content reflects on the experiences of the early years educators about their CPD and how it can be developed effectively. The chapter content considers Kennedy's (2005) 'nine models' of CPD and the importance of transformative CPD in respect of changing the professional experiences of the educators in significant ways. Urban's (2009) critique of the portrayal of early years educators in England as 'solvers of all sorts of problems' is based on the argument that the educators become immersed within a 'game of representation' (Rowbottom and Aiston 2006, 143). There is the implication that the educators ought to go to 'infinity and beyond' so that they become 'super teachers'. As noted earlier in the book, it is Schwandt (2005) who argues convincingly that working with children and families is more about 'the messiness of human life' and less about 'solving problems' (and even less about going to infinity and beyond). In England however, the need to solve problems appears to be a key theme within the framing of CPD in early years (Ingleby 2015). As noted earlier, in the chapter, the theoretical framework that is applied to the research once again considers theories of literacy as social practice where there are 'texts' shaping CPD events that in turn help in generating subjective practices about the benefits or otherwise of these professional development events. CPD in this area is characterised by text-based literacy artefacts (for example the policy documents like the EYFS) producing 'literary events', in other words professional development activities, where as we have previously noted, Tummons (2014, 35) acknowledges that 'literacy has a role'. Alongside these professional development activities there are 'literary practices', that is, the subjective interpretations of professional development within 'social contexts' (Tummons 2014, 36). The content of this chapter applies this epistemological position in interpreting the professional development of early years educators.

CHAPTER RESEARCH CONTEXT

The research explores the experiences of educators in the early years in England who are based in either statutory or private settings. As noted previously, the pedagogy of these practitioners has been shaped by The Every Child Matters agenda via The EYFS, that was essentially introduced in England in 2008 and revised in 2012 (Ingleby 2016). Part of the complexity of this sector of education concerns the fact that in the UK, The EYFS applies to England, however it does not apply to Northern Ireland, Scotland, Wales, Guernsey, Jersey, or The Isle of Man. This results in each jurisdiction of the UK having its own arrangements for childcare and early years education and the associated CPD that these professionals receive varies accordingly. Beijaard et al. (2000) argue that it is important to understand how individual educators process interpretations of CPD if we are to understand how professional development influences professional practice, and yet this complex train of thought does not appear to be shaping CPD in England in general (Eraut 1994). Moreover, this argument certainly appears to apply to the early years in particular.

The themes that are developed within the chapter are relevant for Kennedy's (2005) notion of 'transformative education' and this essentially refers to education that is based on 'the principles of empowerment, social justice, emancipation, and freedom' (McLeod 2015, 256). The work of a number of authors in education is relevant to the chapter themes and these authors include Bers 2008; Hadley et al. 2015; Layen 2015; Lightfoot and Frost 2015; Marklund 2015; McLeod 2015; Perry and MacDonald 2015; Waters and Payler 2015; Winton et al. 2016; and Yelland and Kilderry 2010. This is because these authors consider professional development in early years in other cultural contexts in order to compare and contrast the different approaches to CPD that exist. This literature explores the challenges that are inherent in developing successful professional development with educators in early years and this links to the work of Kennedy (2005) and the reflections that are made about transformative professional development and its importance. It is interesting to consider that 15 years after the publication of Kennedy's (2005) influential article, a key area of debate concerns the strategies that are necessary if we are to witness the occurrence of transformative education, where the experiences of the educators and the students are changed in significant and beneficial ways. The challenges in achieving transformative education in early years are considered by Bers 2008; Hadley et al. 2015; Layen

2015; Lightfoot and Frost 2015; Marklund 2015; McLeod 2015; Perry and MacDonald 2015; Waters and Payler 2015; Winton et al. 2016; and Yelland and Kilderry 2010, and collectively these authors consider two key themes within their work. Reflections are made about the challenges that are present for early years educators in experiencing professional development that is transformative. At the centre of this theme is the argument that there are few forms of CPD that enable early years educators to reflect on how they are developing as professional educators. Some of the challenges that exist within the professional development of early years educators are highlighted by Waters and Payler (2015), and as we have seen already, the definition of these professionals and the sector that they work in is not clear. In England, the professionals who are working in the early years have been referred to as 'the children's workforce' and yet in other cultural contexts, they are described as being 'early years educators' (Waters and Payler 2015, 161). The chapter content applies the term 'early years educators' in order to mirror the consistency of Waters and Payler (2015), and it is worth considering that if the name of the educators is unclear it is also highly unlikely that their plans for effective, transformative CPD will be characterised by a clear philosophy. As we have also seen, the children who qualify to be in this sector of education differ in age according to cultural contexts, so it can be argued that if CPD in early years education is to be transformative, it is vital to ensure that there are neither ambiguities about the definition of the sector of education, nor the children who are included within this educational domain (Hadley et al. 2015; Lightfoot and Frost 2015; McLeod 2015; and Waters and Payler 2015).

A second key theme within the work of the above mentioned authors relates to the provision of CPD that enables the practitioners to reflect on professional practice in ways that transform their work as educators. As McLeod (2015, 255) argues, a mitigating factor concerns the presence of an 'outcome-driven curriculum' that has 'targets imposed by the government as part of a top-down approach' at its centre. This can result in barriers that prevent effective reflection on professional practice. The work of Edwards et al. (2002), and Reed and Canning (2010), also reveals the presence of obstacles in professional practice that work against the development of critical reflections about pedagogy in view of this outcome-driven curriculum. McLeod (2015, 256) argues that an emphasis on achieving an 'end product' in education is more likely to result in what Mezirow (1997) and Jacobs and Murray (2010) refer to as 'oppressing professional customs'. This in turn works against the reflective practice that is advocated by Dewey (1933) and SchÖn (1978), as professional work in this educational sector becomes obscured within educational processes that do not enable 'a critically reflective approach' (McLeod 2015, 256). It is argued that this 'pressure of targets' can in turn work against enabling a sense of transformative education (Dimova and Loughran 2009; Tickell 2011; and Wilkins 2011, cited in McLeod 2015). In consequence, there are experiences producing 'feelings of disillusionment', 'anxiety' and 'loss of control' (Lightfoot and Frost 2015, 401). It is argued that if we are to realise transformative professional development for early years educators, it is important to ensure that professional personal identities are considered in tandem (Hadley et al. 2015; Lightfoot and Frost 2015; McLeod 2015; and Waters and Payler 2015). If we value and appreciate the educators as opposed to 'focusing on outcomes' there emerges the possibility of developing professionals who can make a real difference to the lives of children and their families (Lightfoot and Frost 2015, 415). Moreover Winton et al. (2016) argue for the importance of enabling professional development in order to provide the knowledge, skills and dispositions that are needed if we are to develop high quality learning environments to in turn implement evidence-based practice. In contrast, there appears to be too much professional development that is episodic and disconnected from professional practice. This theme is considered by Marklund (2015) in the argument that the constant newness of technology results in constant change for the sake of change as opposed to the implementation of the effective professional development of early years educators. In contrast, it is the raising of awareness of the processes of learning about professional practice that appears to be necessary if CPD is to become useful in the professional work of early years educators (Layen 2015; Perry and MacDonald 2015). These themes are revealed in the research findings of the chapter and this demonstrates the challenges that are present in implementing effective CPD in this area of education.

THEORETICAL BACKGROUND

The challenges that are involved in the successful professional development of early years educators appear to be based on a combination of subjective and objective factors. There are the policy documents that are shaping this educational context (for example The EYFS) and they can be visualised as being 'literary texts' (Barton 2007; Barton et al. 2000; Gee 1996). In this chapter there is a further conceptualisation of educational sectors being formed via literary texts, the subsequent educational events, and that this in turn realises subjective practices that shape the professional development of the early years educators. It can be argued that the challenges that are present in the effective professional development of early years educators in England are a further example of the manifestation of literacy as social practice.

In the previous chapter about HE in FE we have seen how Barton (2007, 34) argues that literacy is a 'symbolic system used for communication'. In applying this argument, the educational policy documents, for example 'The EYFS', can be visualised as being 'ways of representing the world to others' (Barton 2007, 34). These policy texts in turn establish the basis of 'literary events' that are explained as being 'occasions in everyday life where the written word has a role' (Barton 2007, 35). In England, the professional practice of the early years educators is shaped by policy documents like The EYFS and the curriculum themes within this document (for example 'a unique child', and 'positive relationships'), establish the basis of the texts that in turn inform the CPD activities within this educational sector. Moreover, other texts such as the QAA (Qualification Assurance Agency) benchmark statements for foundation degrees (2010) and early childhood studies (2014), alongside books encouraging 'reflective practice' in early years (for example Lindon 2012) also shape the curriculum events that are enabled by the individuals operating within this context. However, it is important to realise that curriculum events are interpreted according to 'literary practices' and it is Barton (2007, 36) who defines 'literacy practices' as ways of 'using reading and writing in particular situations'. This epistemological understanding of literacies as social practice is once again applied to the book in this chapter in order to explore the relationship that exists in education between the texts, the events and the practices of the educators within their respective professional 'domains' (Barton 2007; Barton et al. 2000; Gee 1996).

KEY RESEARCH FINDINGS

The research findings on professional development in education and early years education reveal three key themes:

1. There are fewer examples of transformative professional development in this form of pedagogy than there ought to be.
2. The early years educational sector in England focuses on 'end products' and results as opposed to nurturing reflection on educational processes and this limits the effectiveness of professional development in this area of education.
3. There is less awareness of developing the personal, social, and professional needs of the early years educators than there ought to be.

1. There are fewer examples of transformative professional development in this form of pedagogy than there ought to be.

Lightfoot and Frost (2015) draw attention to a weakness within the English early years education system by revealing that there are few examples of professional development that are transformative for the professionals who are working in this area of education. In their research, Lightfoot and Frost (2015) explore the nature of the professional identities of nine early years educators. The research reveals the sheer complexity of factors that combine together in intricate ways to shape the identities of the educators. It is argued by Lightfoot and Frost (2015) that professional development in education in this area cannot simply focus on the duties and the responsibilities of these educators if it is to become truly transformational. This is because it is important to ensure that professional development takes place in ways that reveal how much the educators are valued as individuals so that they are enabled to make an effective difference in their professional practice. If this sense of transformative professional development is to occur in early years education in England, Lightoot and Frost (2015) argue that a number of key factors ought to be worked into the future planning of professional development in this area. These factors include ensuring that external expertise is based on early years based activities; and that this experience is used to develop reflection, planning, and experimentation. Moreover, the development of encouraging, extending, and structuring professional dialogue holds the potential to become a means of enabling effective professional development in this area of education.

Waters and Payler (2015) also argue that there is less transformative and systemic change in the early years education system in England than there ought to be. It is argued by Waters and Payler (2015) that if we are to explore whether or not professional development in early years education in England is transformative, we need to consider what is distinctive about what is occurring. Waters and Payler (2015) draw on the work of Ball (2013) to argue that there is tension inherent in the professional development of educators in the early years because of neoliberalism. It is Ball (2013) who reveals that early years educators are influenced in their professional practice by neoliberal concerns with ensuring that their professional practice is part of a global project that ensures economic productivity and competitiveness. This is similar to the argument from Urban (2009) that positions early years educators as being akin to being interpreted as being solvers of problems. Waters and Payler (2015) reveal that the emphasis that has been placed upon improving the quality of early years educators has indirectly resulted in difficulties in ensuring that transformative professional development is occurring in this sector of education. There appears to be a focus being placed on ensuring that there are vocationally qualified educators operating in this sphere of education, however the achievement of qualifications in itself does not lead to transformative professional development (Kennedy 2005). As Urban (2009) argues, it is what results from these qualifications that is important and in England it can be argued that there has been little thought given to transformative professional development in the early years by the English neoliberal policymakers.

Davies and Head (2010) argue that transformative professional development in the early years ought not be as significant a challenge as it appears to be. It is argued that collaboration is particularly important in early years education and that if this experience of collaboration is enabled, this in turn holds the potential to nurture a full sense of transformative professional development. Davies and Head (2010) argue that this sense of collaboration is evident in partnerships that have developed between learners and educators in the early years. The transformation of the idea that an educator is somehow a 'leader' of education that has emerged through pedagogical philosophies such as Montessori, Reggio Emilia, and Steiner has challenged traditional hierarchical and linear models of pedagogy in the early years and fostered a greater awareness of the importance of collaboration. Davies and Head (2010, 339) argue that the consequence of this new pedagogy has resulted in examples where academics and educators come together as a 'local community' that 'starts with the child'. It is argued that this in turn enables the development of critical thinking and cooperative learning that is in turn able to focus on a pedagogy of relationships. Davies and Head (2010, 350) argue that ultimately the importance of 'sharing interactions' and 'sharing practice' is at the centre of developing transformative professional development, however, in England there are other agendas that have become detrimental to this experience of transformative professional development. The early years education system in England is intrinsically linked to the primary education system and in consequence, this mitigates against a focus on collaboration and sharing practice because what is happening in England links to an educational agenda that is beyond the early years (Urban 2009).

If we are to realise an experience of transformative professional development in the early years in England, it is important that we learn from what appears to be working in other cultural contexts in this area. Philippou et al. (2015) reveal some of the benefits of transformative professional development in the early years by presenting their research findings on developing inquiry-based approaches to mathematics and science-based education in the early years. Philippou et al. (2015) argue, like Davies and Head (2010) that professional development that nurtures inquiry-based pedagogical approaches enables the educators to focus on processes of pedagogy, as opposed to having to deal with agendas that are beyond their immediate professional practice. Philippou et al. (2015) argue that it is important to develop a community of educational practice that enables a transformative focus on the purpose of pedagogy in the early years. By uniting 'theory' with 'practice' it becomes possible to ensure that as much of the educational process as possible is based on enabling inquiry-based forms of pedagogy (Philippou et al. 2015, 382). Philippou et al. (2015) acknowledge that if we are to have a sense of transformative professional development in early years education it is important to move away from a notion of 'consuming' knowledge and instead focus upon the 'production' of knowledge. Once again, this argument is based on reflecting on the processes of pedagogy as opposed to looking at what is produced by processes of knowledge generation. This also appears to enable educators to reflect on the nature of their roles in the early years and Philippou et al. (2015) propose that this aspect of education is at the centre of transformational professional development in education in the early years.

2. The early years educational sector in England focuses on 'end products' and results as opposed to nurturing reflection on educational processes and this limits the effectiveness of professional development in this area of education.

Previously, reference has been made to Urban's (2009) reflection that educators in the early years in England can be perceived as being solvers of problems. There is a focus on end products and solutions to problems via obtaining demonstrable results and this can work against effective professional development in education. Anning (2005) strengthens this argument by reflecting on the neoliberal establishment of UK Centres of Excellence by the DfES. These UK Centres of Excellence were the precursors to the Children's Centres that were introduced across the UK and the philosophy behind the establishment of these Children's Centres is based on the rhetoric that multi-agency team work will make a difference to the lives of children and families. However, Anning (2005, 43) reveals that multi-agency teams bring 'a diversity of knowledge, beliefs, and values' to professional practice and that this can work against the development of coherent effective processes of working and the subsequent CPD that is necessary to develop professional practice effectively. It appears to be the case that neoliberal governments in England have considered that the establishment of these 'Children's Centres' is an inevitable good in its own right when the reality of the processes of professional work with children and families involves asking early years practitioners 'to operate at a highly sophisticated level in juggling the competing demands of their traditional, professional values/beliefs with each other and at the same time with those of their host communities' (Anning 2005, 43).

Potter (2007) also argues that here is a tendency by neoliberal governments in England to focus on end-products and that this is revealed in particular with regards to the establishment of the EYFS and the 'EYP' (Early Years Professional) role. In consequence this has obscured the 'rigorous conceptual underpinnings' that are necessary if effective professional practice and its subsequent forms of professional development are to be established (Potter 2007, 171). It is argued by Potter (2007, 177) that if we are to improve children's language and communications development in England, it is necessary to develop 'detailed knowledge and understanding not only of how language and communication develops but also of the strategies most likely to promote it'. This focus on 'processes' as opposed to the establishment of 'products' appears to be a missing ingredient in the development of effective professional development for educators in the early years in the neoliberal English context. The establishment of 'an informed developmental framework' is thus advocated as being a means of moving this agenda forward in the early years in England (Potter 2007, 178). The advantage of focusing on pedagogical processes is considered by Potter (2007, 178) to be significant because this will then in turn enable the emergence of 'practitioners with specific in-depth knowledge of the development of language and communication and strategies for promoting it in early years settings'.

Linklater (2006) also argues for the importance of moving away from focusing on 'end products' and instead studying the pedagogical processes that are important for educators who are working in the early years. In particular, it is argued by Linklater (2006) that it is important to listen to children if we are to learn from them and subsequently develop our professional practice in the early years. Linklater (2006) refers to the establishment of the 'QCA' (Qualifications Curriculum Authority) 'early learning goals' and 'curriculum guidance for the foundation stage' in England from 1999–2000. It is argued by Linklater (2006) that children's experiences in education are not informing these end product documents as effectively as they should do because there appear to be few examples where children are valued as being potential participants in the research that is informing neoliberal policies and the subsequent professional development that is necessary to implement these policies. Linklater (2006, 76) argues that if 'children's voices' are heard, this can enable the development of an understanding of 'the shared social and cultural contexts' that inform pedagogical processes in the early years'.

Mathers et al. (2007) argue that the understandings of 'quality' educational provision by neoliberal governments in England can be problematic because these specific understandings of this term can be challenged by other differing interpretations of what 'quality' should actually refer to. In exemplifying this argument 'quality' could be interpreted as referring to 'issues of access and inclusion' (Mathers et al. 2007, 272), and the single terms that are used frequently to explain 'quality' education in early years in England 'only ever cover a limited spectrum' as opposed to considering the experiences of individual children (Mathers et al. 2007, 72). Mathers et al. (2007) also argue for the importance of ensuring that the training that is necessary to ensure that interpretations of quality in the early years in England are reliable and consistent is addressed effectively. There are examples in this book (for example in Chap. 5), where 'quality' appears to 'become a stick' that is used to 'beat' educators and it is argued by Mathers et al. (2007, 72) that interpretations of quality ought to be used in ways that are 'sensitive and appropriate' alongside encouraging 'a process of reflective self-evaluation'.

3. There is less awareness of developing the personal, social, and professional needs of the early years educators than there ought to be.

Ingleby (2016), and Ingleby and Wilford (2016), and Ingleby et al. (2019) reflect on the challenges that exist for educators in education in England in respect of the professional development opportunities that are made available to develop pedagogy. This work is once again informed by Kennedy (2005) in considering the occurrence of transformative professional development in education. It is argued that there are few forms of professional development that transform the educators in respect of their personal, social, and professional needs. Ingleby (2016) reveals that educators in the early years do not simply replicate the desired outcomes of the neoliberal policymakers because there are subjective and organisational factors at work in the assessment of whether or not the policy recommendations are worth following. Although the neoliberal policymakers recommend the application of technology to pedagogy in England in the early years, this does not automatically mean that the recommendation will occur in professional practice. Ingleby (2016) reveals the importance of subjective factors influencing the professional development of educators alongside considering other organisational factors that may influence the experience of CPD (for example, the nature of the early years setting and the professional pressures that are being experienced). It is argued that these subjective and organisational factors are important in respect of shaping the educators' interpretations about CPD.

Ingleby and Wilford (2016), and Ingleby et al. (2019) develop the argument that subjective and organisational factors are important in influencing professional development in education by arguing that a complex combination of personal, social, and professional needs influence the perceptions of professional development that are present in minds of the educators. In applying Kennedy's (2005) work, it is argued that there are many forms of professional development in England where an assumption is made that the educators are lacking a particular skill and that the role of CPD is to fill the gap that exists in respect of this missing skill. This is essentially what Kennedy (2005) reflects on with her 'deficit' model of CPD. However, it is argued by Ingleby and Wilford (2016) and Ingleby et al. (2019) that CPD is influenced by a complex combination of the personal, social, and professional needs of the educators. In exemplifying this argument, if a CPD session on the principles of the Reggio Emilia approach to teaching and learning is made available to educators in the early years, the uptake of this CPD session will be influenced by the personal, social, and professional circumstances of the educators. There are the 'personal' dispositions of the educators that affect whether or not this CPD opportunity is utilised that are dependent upon 'personal' like or dislike of the Reggio Emilia approach to pedagogy. There are also 'social' factors that influence how this professional development opportunity is realised or not realised. The Reggio Emilia approach to pedagogy is not known well in the state education system in England, so this lack of social awareness of the pedagogical approach is also likely to influence whether or not the CPD opportunity is used. The individual 'professional' perceptions of the educators will also influence the responses to professional development opportunities. If an educator in the early years in England is working with those children beyond preschool age, this will influence the motivation being expressed towards utilising this CPD opportunity in this 'Reggio Emilia' example. If the personal, social, and professional characteristics of the educators are taken into consideration in the design of CPD programmes this will in turn become a potential means whereby professional development becomes transformative, in view of the cogent rationale that is informing the subsequent development of CPD.

The arguments of Ingleby and Wilford (2016), and Ingleby et al. (2019) also apply to the work of Perry and MacDonald (2015) where it is acknowledged that personal, subjective factors influence the successful implementation of CPD. The educators' 'beliefs and attitudes' in respect of their 'expectations and aspirations' appear to be critical factors that need to be taken into consideration if professional development in education is to be helpful. However, it is evident that there is less awareness of these factors than there ought to be in professional development in education in England.

Concluding Discussion

The research in this chapter presents complex challenges in respect of CPD for educators in the early years in England and the research findings have wider implications for professional development in education. There are a number of academics who focus on the complex processes of professional development including Harland and Kinder (2014), Leask and Younie (2013), Loughran (2006), and Macfarlane and Cartmel (2012), however the richness that is present in this body of work does not seem to be influencing neoliberal approaches to developing professional development in education as extensively as it ought to. This is because this collective academic work situates the challenges of professional development in education within the processes that are enabled if we are to see effective CPD. In this chapter it is revealed that the focus on 'end products' can result in professional development in education becoming a low priority and that when CPD opportunities are available, they are not necessarily supportive of the personal, social, and professional development needs of the educators. It appears to be the case that the wider concerns of neoliberal governments in England (for example the commercial priorities of the private settings, the pressures to meet teaching targets, and the impact of Ofsted) can appear to be mitigating factors that affect the successful implementation of CPD in England.

In complementing the research of Harland and Kinder (2014), Leask and Younie (2013), Loughran (2006), and Macfarlane and Cartmel (2012); it is helpful to regard professional development in education via an epistemological interpretation of theories of literacy as social practice. The experience of professional development in education is established through the relationship that exists between 'texts', curriculum 'events' and pedagogical 'practices' (Ingleby and Gibby 2016). The educators are influenced by the neoliberal policymakers and their 'texts', for example The EYFS, and the government documents that appear via Ofsted with their subsequent emphasis being placed upon meeting targets. It can be argued that the professional development 'events' that are experienced by the early years educators in England have their origins in these 'texts' (Barton 2007; Barton et al. 2000; Gee 1996). The individual subjective 'practices' about these CPD events are revealed in the statements that are made about professional development that are captured in the research that is occurring on professional development in education. In considering exploring the texts, events and practices that are informing professional development in education it becomes possible to gain insights into some of the challenges that are present in developing CPD in England. The reflections of the research participants in the published research on CPD in this area reveal how subjective practices are informed by the texts that generate formal CPD within this context. If we are to understand 'practices' it is important to take into consideration the 'texts' and 'events' that influence what is unfolding in this particular educational context (Barton 2007). The policy documents influencing early years in England (for example The EYFS, The QAA Foundation Degree Benchmarks 2010, and The QAA Subject Statements for Early Childhood Studies 2014) shape the subsequent CPD events that are in turn interpreted as social practices by the educators (Barton 2007; Barton et al. 2000; and Gee 1996). The early years educators in the research reflect on the nature of professional practice and how this impacts on their own experience of CPD and the collective angst that is expressed by the educators is in general about experiences that they consider to work against the effective development of pedagogy in this area of education. It is the texts that are defining the nature of the CPD events and this is subsequently influencing professional experiences. The research in this chapter has revealed that these texts need to be written differently by neoliberal policymakers. The research reveals that the personal, social, and professional needs of the educators have to be taken into consideration in the design of CPD programmes. This is the key message in the work of Ingleby and Wilford (2016) and Ingleby et al. (2019). If this development can occur, this will in turn help in enabling forms of CPD that are based on sound philosophies of pedagogy. By taking the personal, social, and professional characteristics of the educators into consideration, this will potentially enable the emergence of holistic forms of professional development. However, if this is to happen the current way of managing education in England by neoliberal governments will need to be changed dramatically.

REFERENCES

Anning, A. 2005. Investigating the impact of working in multi-agency service delivery settings in the UK on early years practitioners' beliefs and practices. *Journal of Early Childhood Research* 3 (1): 19–50.

Ball, S.J. 2013. *The education debate.* 2nd ed. Bristol: The Policy Press.

Barton, D. 2007. *Literacy: An introduction to the ecology of written language.* Oxford: Blackwell Publishing.

Barton, D., M. Hamilton, and R. Ivanič. 2000. *Situated literacies: Reading and writing in context.* London: Routledge.

Beijaard, D., N. Verloop, and J.D. Vermunt. 2000. Teachers' perceptions of professional identity: An exploratory study from a personal knowledge perspective. *Teaching and Teacher Education* 16: 749–764.

Bers, M. 2008. *Blocks to robots: Learning with technology in the early childhood classroom.* New York: Teachers College Press.

Davies, H., and C. Head. 2010. Pedagogical exchange for professional development: Reflections on how collaboration has inspired and empowered a group of early years educators to find new ways of working to improve learning and teaching. *The International Journal of Learning* 17 (9): 339–352.

Dewey, J. 1933. *How we think: A restatement of the relation of reflective thinking in the educative process.* New York: Health and Company.

Dimova, Y., and J. Loughran. 2009. Developing a big picture understanding of reflection in pedagogical practice. *Reflective Practice* 10 (2): 205–217.

Edwards, A., P. Gilroy, and D. Hartley. 2002. *Rethinking teacher education: Collaborative responses to uncertainty.* London: Routledge Falmer.

Eraut, M. 1994. *Developing professional knowledge and competence.* London: Falmer Press.

Gee, J.P. 1996. *Social linguistics and literacies.* London: Routledge Falmer.

Hadley, F., M. Waniganiyake, and W. Shepherd. 2015. Contemporary practice in professional learning and development of early years educators in Australia: Reflections on what works and why. *Professional Development in Education* 41 (2): 187–203.

Harland, J., and K. Kinder. 2014. Teachers' continuing professional development: Framing a model of outcomes. *Professional Development in Education* 40 (4): 669–682.

Ingleby, E. 2015. The impact of changing policies about technology on the professional development needs of early years educators in England. *Professional Development in Education* 41 (1): 144–158.

———. 2016. We don't just do what we're told to do! Practitioner perceptions of using ICTs in early years. *International Journal of Early Years Education* 24 (1): 36–48.

Ingleby, E., and C. Gibby. 2016. Law and ethics: Problematising the role of the foundation degree and paralegal education in English post-compulsory education. *Research in Post-compulsory Education* 21 (1–2): 151–163.

Ingleby, E., and B. Wilford. 2016. Pedagogy with technology in higher education in England. A brave new world? Paper presented at the IPDA conference, 25–26 November, Birmingham, UK.

Ingleby, E., B. Wilford, and C. Hedges. 2019. Teaching with technology and higher education: A brave new world? *Practice: Contemporary Issues in Practitioner Education* 1 (1): 73–87.

Jacobs, G., and M. Murray. 2010. Developing critical understanding by teaching action research to undergraduate psychology students. *Educational Action Research* 18 (3): 319–335.

Kennedy, A. 2005. Models of CPD: A framework for analysis. *Journal of In-service Education* 31 (2): 235–250.

Layen, S. 2015. Do reflections on personal autobiography as captured in narrated life-stories illuminate leadership development in the field of early childhood. *Professional Development in Education* 41 (2): 254–273.

Leask, M., and S. Younie. 2013. National models for continuing professional development: The challenges of twenty first century knowledge management. *Professional Development in Education* 39 (2): 273–287.

Lightfoot, S., and D. Frost. 2015. The professional identity of early years educators in England: Implications for a transformative approach to continuing professional development. *Professional Development in Education* 41 (2): 401–418.

Lindon, J. 2012. *Reflective practice and early years professionalism.* 2nd ed. London: Hodder Education.

Linklater, H. 2006. Listening to learn: Children playing and talking about the reception year of early years education in the UK. *Early Years* 26 (1): 63–78.

Loughran, J. 2006. *Developing a pedagogy of teacher education: Understanding teaching and learning about teaching.* Abingdon: Routledge.

Macfarlane, K., and J. Cartmel. 2012. Circles of change revisited: Building leadership, scholarship and professional identity in the children's services sector. *Professional Development in Education* 38 (5): 845–861.

Marklund, L. 2015. Preschool teachers' informal online professional development in relation to educational use of tablets in Swedish preschools. *Professional Development in Education* 41 (2): 236–253.

Mathers, S., F. Linksey, J. Seddon, and K. Sylva. 2007. Using quality rating scales for professional development: Experiences from the UK. *International Journal of Early Years Education* 15 (3): 261–2714.

McLeod, N. 2015. Reflecting on reflection: Improving teachers' readiness to facilitate participatory learning with young children. *Professional Development in Education* 41 (2): 254–273.

Mezirow, J. 1997. Transformative learning: Theory to practice. In *Transformative learning in action: Insights from practice: New directions for adult and continuing education*, ed. P. Cranton, 5–12. San Francisco, CA: Jossey-Bass.

Nutbrown, C. 2012. *Foundations for quality: The independent review of early education and childcare qualifications.* London: Department for Education.

Perry, B., and M. MacDonald. 2015. Educators' expectations and aspirations around young children's mathematical knowledge. *Professional Development in Education* 41 (2): 336–382.

Philippou, S., C. Papademetri-Kachrimani, and L. Louca. 2015. 'The exchange of ideas was mutual, I have to say': Negotiating researcher and teacher 'roles' in an early years educators' professional development programme on inquiry-based mathematics and science learning. *Professional Development in Education* 41 (2): 382–400.

Potter, C.A. 2007. Developments in UK early years policy and practice: Can they improve outcomes for disadvantaged children? *International Journal of Early Years Education* 15 (2): 171–180.

Quality Assurance Authority. 2010. *Foundation degree qualification benchmark.* Gloucester: Quality Assurance Agency for Higher Education.

———. 2014. *Subject benchmark statement: Early childhood studies.* Gloucester: Quality Assurance Agency for Higher Education.

Reed, M., and N. Canning. 2010. *Reflective practice in the early years.* London: Sage.

Rowbottom, D.P., and S.J. Aiston. 2006. The myth of 'scientific method' in contemporary educational research. *Journal of Philosophy of Education* 40 (2): 137–156.

SchÖn, D.A. 1978. *Educating the reflective practitioner: Toward a new design for teaching.* San Francisco, CA: Jossey-Bass.

Schwandt, T.A. 2005. *A diagnostic of scientifically based research for education.* Malden, MA: Blackwell.

Tickell, C. 2011. *The early years: Foundations for life, health and learning: An independent report on the early years foundation stage to her Majesty's government.* London: Department for Education.

Tummons, J.E. 2014. The textual representation of professionalism: Problematising professional standards for teachers in the UK lifelong learning sector. *Research in Post-compulsory Education* 19 (1): 33–44.

Urban, M. 2009. Strategies for change: rethinking professional development to meet the challenges of diversity in the early years profession. Paper presented at the IPDA conference, 27–28 November, Birmingham, UK.

Waller, T. 2005. *An introduction to early childhood: A multidisciplinary approach.* London: Paul Chapman.

Waters, J., and J. Payler. 2015. The professional development of early years educators- achieving systematic, sustainable and transformative change. *Professional Development in Education* 41 (2): 161–169.

Wilkins, C. 2011. Professionalism and the post-performative teacher: New teachers reflect on autonomy and accountability in the English school system. *Professional Development in Education* 37 (3): 389–409.

Winton, P., P. Snyder, and S. Goffin. 2016. Beyond the status-quo: Rethinking professional development for early childhood teachers. In *Handbook of early childhood teacher education,* ed. L. Couse and S. Recchia, 54–68. New York: Routledge.

Yelland, N., and A. Kilderry. 2010. Becoming numerate with information technologies in the twenty-first century. *International Journal of Early Years Education* 18 (2): 91–106.

CHAPTER 8

Conclusion

In education, as a discipline there are always potentially interesting conversational topics, and this is certainly the case with neoliberalism and its influence on education in England. This book draws on research projects in education that have taken place from 2006–2017 and covered a full range of educational contexts, ranging from the early years to higher education. The research provides insights into educational settings that are rich and varied and the conversations that are occurring in these educational spaces in England are a product of the influence of neoliberalism. In this book we have seen that in neoliberalism there is a contradiction occurring in the belief that the government should not intervene directly in health, care, and education, unless it has to, alongside subsequently witnessing multiple examples where neoliberal governments have intervened directly and made changes in education. The academy schools in England are one example where this neoliberal intervention is evidenced. In applying the work of Urban (2009) and Vermunt (2016) to the chapters of the book, we have seen that these interventions in education are not necessarily informed by professional expertise in education. There is a fascinating occurrence of interventions in education being influenced by factors that are beyond education, including economic and political agendas that appear to be the central concerns for neoliberal governments in England.

The reframing of education in England by neoliberal governments is akin to a game of representation where the changes in interpretation of

© The Author(s), under exclusive license to Springer Nature   131
Switzerland AG 2021
E. Ingleby, *Neoliberalism Across Education*, Palgrave Studies on
Global Policy and Critical Futures in Education,
https://doi.org/10.1007/978-3-030-73962-1_8

the purpose of education are expressed via fascinating discourse. This has been revealed in the pandemic in 2020 in England when one of the first groups of children to return to primary schools after the national lockdown were those children aged four to five years of age in reception classes. There appeared to be no discernible educational reason for this return to education for these children and perhaps this decision was based on the belief that employees could not return to work if they were home-schooling 'needy' four to five year old children, and that this would damage the economy? This decision was taken by the neoliberal Conservative administration in England in 2020 and the view that schools are places where children should be 'looked after' appears to have informed this political decision. In contrast, in the philosophies of education that have been considered in this book, the Montessori, Reggio Emilia, and Steiner approaches to education enable children to direct learning processes, and this appears to be of benefit to the children in respect of their subsequent physical, intellectual, emotional, and social development. However, in England, in consequence of neoliberal governments, there can be the occurrence of what Hayes and Ecclestone (2019) refer to as 'therapeutic education'. Hayes and Ecclestone (2019) argue that in England education does not work and that this is why we talk about education all of the time. It is argued by Hayes and Ecclestone (2019) that a sense of disorientation about the purpose of education coincides with what society ought to expect from children, and that the portrayal of children as being somehow vulnerable and at risk has led to the emergence of therapeutic education, where the learners are portrayed in ways that are the opposite of those philosophies of education that encourage child led pedagogy.

This theme of the misinterpretation of education is at the centre of each of the main chapters of this book. In considering the application of technology to early years education in England it is revealed that neoliberal governments in England are obsessed with applying technology to pedagogy by assuming that 'e is best' without reflecting on the pedagogical processes and the associated professional development in education that is essential if technology is to be applied effectively to pedagogy. It is revealed that although interventions in education have occurred to make technology a key part of the early years curriculum, the complex personal, social, and professional factors influencing this form of pedagogy have not been considered fully. In Chap. 3, this theme of underdeveloped philosophical considerations about education is also revealed. The neoliberal policymakers in England have produced an education system that focuses on 'results' and this has led to less emphasis being given to the actual pedagogical processes that are occurring in primary and secondary schools in England. The focus on educational results has led to what can be measured and quantified becoming important in schools in England and this has consequences for the development of creative thinking strategies in these educational contexts. In Chap. 4 it is revealed that neoliberal interventions in secondary schools in England have consequences for tertiary education. The perception of a 'further education system' in England that is for 'vocational education' has been transformed by the introduction of 'self-regulating' academy schools that are able to mirror agendas that were once the preserve of the tertiary education sector. In consequence it is argued that the academy schools are not merely imitating the vocational objectives of the tertiary sector as there is the occurrence of the tertiary sector blending together with the academy schools in ways that are hyper-real. Chapter 5 considers the intervention by neoliberal policymakers into the FE system in England by considering how perceptions of mentoring have been shaped into judging the performance of educators. The content reveals that whereas the educators prefer a mentoring system that is supportive and non-judgemental alongside being informed by a clear philosophy of education, the neoliberal policymakers have created a form of mentoring that assesses professional performance so that 'effectiveness' can in turn be quantified and measured. The chapter reveals that education in England can be interpreted as being constituted of 'texts' (formal policy documents that recommend what should happen in education), alongside 'events' (curriculum activities that are shaped by these texts), and 'practices' (that represent subjective, personal interpretations of texts and events). This theme is also applied to the final two chapters of the book. It is argued that HE in FE in England can be understood as being a product of a complex interplay between the neoliberal policy texts that result in curriculum activities and the subsequent personal interpretations of this form of higher education. The advantage of applying literacy as social practice to education in England is revealed when the disconnect between policy and practice is illuminated. This appears to be a characteristic of professional development in education in England and this is considered in the final main chapter of the book. The policy documents about CPD in England do not appear to be producing activities that are making the educators experience a sense of what Kennedy (2005) refers to as transformative professional development. As opposed to enabling professional led CPD, professional development in England is characterised by an absence of coherent thought in general, and it is argued that this is a direct consequence of neoliberal governments' inadequacy in developing educational contexts in England effectively.

Alongside the absence of coherent philosophies of education that are informing early years, primary, secondary, tertiary, and higher education in England, there are also a number of key social challenges that are impacting upon the nurturing and development of the English educational contexts. According to statistics from 'Age UK', there are now nearly 12 million people aged over 65 years in the UK and the financial needs of these individuals lessens the resources that are available for educational contexts (www.guardian.com.uk). There are also financial challenges for the education sector in England due to the £1 trillion that has been committed to reducing greenhouse gas emissions, and the years of underinvestment in the wider infrastructure that characterises the 'ambition of absence' of neoliberal governments in England (www.guardian.com.uk). Moreover, the UK has evidenced a lost decade of productivity following the financial crisis of 2008, and there are currently only 825 homes per 1000 families, the lowest number since records began in 1991 (www.guardian.com.uk). These social challenges are hardly likely to encourage neoliberal governments in England to invest in the education system as much as is necessary if there is to be an effective development of English educational contexts. Alongside these demographic and infrastructure challenges, there are also acute social problems in England. There are difficulties caused by violent crime, drug use, and domestic abuse that have exacerbated over time in England, and this draws resources away from developing educational contexts effectively (www.guardian.com.uk). In consequence, Tony Blair's famous mantra of 'education, education, education' under neoliberal policymakers can be argued to have actually resulted in 'problems, problems, problems'. What will the future hold?

References

Hayes, D., and K. Ecclestone. 2019. *The dangerous rise of therapeutic education.* Oxford: Routledge.

Kennedy, A. 2005. Models of CPD: A framework for analysis. *Journal of In-service Education* 31 (2): 235–250.

Urban, M. 2009. Strategies for change: rethinking professional development to meet the challenges of diversity in the early years profession. Paper presented at the IPDA conference, 27–28 November, Birmingham, UK.

Vermunt, J.D. 2016. Keynote address. Paper presented at the IPDA conference, 25–26 November, Stirling, UK.

REFERENCES

Abbas, A., P. Ashwin, and M. McLean. 2012. Neoliberal policy, quality and inequality in undergraduate degrees. In *Organising neoliberalism: Markets, privatisation and injustice*, ed. P. Crawshaw and P. Whitehead, 181–199. London: Anthem Press.

Alred, G., B. Garvey, and R. Smith. 1998. *Mentoring pocketbook*. Alresford: Management Pocketbooks.

Andersen, N.A. 2003. *Discursive analytical strategies: Understanding Foucault, Koselleck, Laclau, Luhmann*. Bristol: Policy Press.

Anderson, E.M., and A. Shannon. 1988. Towards a conceptualisation of mentoring. *Journal of Teacher Education* 39 (1): 38–42.

Anning, A. 2005. Investigating the impact of working in multi-agency service delivery settings in the UK on early years practitioners' beliefs and practices. *Journal of Early Childhood Research* 3 (1): 19–50.

Apple, M. 2001. Comparing neo-liberal projects and inequality in education. *Comparative Education* 37 (4): 409–423.

Archer, L., and C. Leathwood. 2003. Identities and inequalities in higher education. In *Higher education and social class: Issues of exclusion and inclusion*, ed. L. Archer, M. Hutchings, and A. Ross, 176–191. London: Routledge Falmer.

Association of Colleges. n.d.-a Accessed July 1, 2015. http://www.aoc.co.uk/.

———. n.d.-b Accessed July 21, 2016. http://www.aoc.co.uk/.

Association of Teachers and Lecturers (ATL). 2017. Accessed October 3, 2018. https://www.atl.org.uk/latest/atl-survey-finds-support-staff-increasingly-having-teach-lessons.

© The Author(s), under exclusive license to Springer Nature Switzerland AG 2021
E. Ingleby, *Neoliberalism Across Education*, Palgrave Studies on Global Policy and Critical Futures in Education, https://doi.org/10.1007/978-3-030-73962-1

135

Atkins, L. 2013. From marginal learning to marginal employment? The real impact of learning employability skills. *Power and Education* 5 (1): 28–37.

Audi, R. 1995. *The Cambridge dictionary of philosophy*. Cambridge: Cambridge University Press.

Bagley, C.A., and C.L. Ackerley. 2006. 'I am much more than just a mum'. Social capital, empowerment and sure start. *Journal of Education Policy* 21 (6): 717–734.

Ball, S. 1998. Performativity and fragmentation in the education economy: Towards the performative society? *Australian Educational Researcher* 27 (2): 1–23.

Ball, S.J. 2005. Radical policies, progressive modernisation and deepening democracy: The academies programme in action. *Forum* 47 (2 & 3): 215–222.

Ball, S. 2010. New class inequalities in education. Why education policy may be looking in the wrong place! Education policy, civil society and social class. *International Journal of Sociology and Social Policy* 30 (3–4): 155–166.

Ball, S.J. 2013. *The education debate*. 2nd ed. Bristol: The Policy Press.

Barnett, R. 1992. *Improving higher education: Total quality care*. Buckingham: SRHE and Open University Press.

———. 2011. The marketised university: Defending the indefensible. In *The marketisation of higher education and the student as consumer*, ed. M. Molesworth, R. Scullion, and E. Nixon, 39–51. Abingdon: Routledge.

Barton, D. 2007. *Literacy: An introduction to the ecology of written language*. Oxford: Blackwell Publishing.

Barton, D., M. Hamilton, and R. Ivanić. 2000. *Situated literacies: Reading and writing in context*. London: Routledge.

Bathmaker, A.M., and J. Avis. 2005. Becoming a lecturer in further education in England: The construction of professional identity and the role of communities of practice. *The Journal of Education for Teaching* 31 (1): 47–62.

Baudrillard, J. 1983. *Simulations*. London: MIT Press.

———. 1993. *Symbolic exchange and death*. London: Sage.

Beijaard, D., N. Verloop, and J.D. Vermunt. 2000. Teachers' perceptions of professional identity: An exploratory study from a personal knowledge perspective. *Teaching and Teacher Education* 16: 749–764.

Bernstein, B. 2000. *Pedagogy, symbolic control and identity*. Lanham, MD: Rowman and Littlefield.

Bers, M. 2008. *Blocks to robots: Learning with technology in the early childhood classroom*. New York: Teachers College Press.

Biesta, G.J.J. 2006. *Beyond learning. Democratic education for a human future*. Boulder, CO: Paradigm Publishers.

Blair, T. 2004. The prime minister's speech to the IPPR think tank and Universities UK joint conference on higher education reform, 14 January in London.

Blunkett, D. 2000. Greenwich speech. Department for Education and Employment. Accessed July 20, 2019. http://www.cms1.gre.ac.uk/dfee/#speech.

Brookes, W. 2005. The graduate teacher programme in England: Mentor training, quality assurance and the findings of inspection. *Journal of In-service Education* 31 (1): 43–61.

Brown, C., Y. Lan, and H. In Jeong. 2015. Beginning to entangle the strange coupling of power within a neoliberal early education context. *International Journal of Early Years Education* 23 (2): 138–152.

Browne, J. 2010. *Securing a sustainable suture for higher education: An independent review of higher education funding and student finance.* London: UK Government.

Bryan, H., and C. Carpenter. 2008. Mentoring: A practice developed in community. *Journal of In-service Education* 34 (1): 47–59.

Burbules, N.C. 1986. A theory of power in education. *Educational Theory* 36 (2): 95–114.

Burkill, S., S. Rodway-Dyer, and M. Stone. 2008. Lecturing in higher education in further education settings. *Journal of Further and Higher Education* 32 (4): 321–331.

Burton, K., M. Lloyd, and C. Griffiths. 2012. Barriers to learning for mature students studying HE in an FE college. *Journal of Further and Higher Education* 35 (1): 25–36.

Caldwell, B.J. 2010. The impact of high-stakes test-driven accountability. *Professional Voice* 8 (1): 49–55.

Caldwell, B.J., and J. Harris. 2008. *Why not the best schools?* Camberwell: Acer Press.

Carmichael, P., and R. Procter. 2006. IT for education research: Using new technology to enhance a complex research programme. London: Institute of Education. Accessed July 20, 2019. http://www.tlrp.org/pub/documents/no16_procter.pdf.

Chapman, C. 2011. Academy federations, chains, and teaching schools in England: Reflections on leadership, policy, and practice. *Journal of School Choice* 7 (3): 334–352.

Clarke, P. 2014. *Report into allegations concerning Birmingham schools arising from 'Trojan Horse' letter.* London: HMSO.

Clegg, S., A. Hudson, and J. Steel. 2003. The emperor's new clothes: Globalisation and e-learning in higher education. *British Journal of Sociology of Education* 24 (1): 39–53.

Coffield, F. 2004. *Learning styles and pedagogy in post-16 learning; a systematic and critical review.* London: The Learning and Skills Research Centre.

———. 2006a. From the decade of enterprise culture to the decade of the TECs. *British Journal of Education and Work* 4 (1): 59–78.

———. 2006b. *Running ever faster down the wrong road,* Inaugural Lecture. London: London University Institute of Education.

Coldron, J., and R. Smith. 1999. Active location in teachers' construction of their professional identities. *Journal of Curriculum Studies* 31 (4): 711–726.

Colley, H. 2003. *Mentoring for social inclusion: A critical approach to nurturing mentor relationships.* London: Routledge.

Colmer, K., M. Waniganayake, and L. Field. 2015. Implementing curriculum reform: Insights into how Australian early childhood directors view professional development and learning. *Professional Development in Education* 41 (2): 203–221.

Conservative Party Manifesto. 2015. Strong leadership, a clear economic plan, a brighter more secure future. Accessed June 1, 2015. https://www.conservatives.com/Manifesto.

———. 2017. Forward together: our plan for a stronger Britain and a more prosperous future. Accessed October 9, 2017. https://www.conservatives.com/Manifesto.

———. 2019. Get brexit done unleash Britain's potential. Accessed November 25, 2019. https://feweek.co.uk/wp-content/uploads/2019/11/Conservative2019Manifesto.pdf.

Craft, A., T. Cremin, P. Burnard, T. Dragovic, and K. Chappell. 2013. Possibility thinking: Culminative studies of an evidence based concept driving creativity? *International Journal of Primary, Elementary and Early Years Education* 41 (5): 3–13.

Creasy, R. 2013. HE lite: Exploring the problematic position of HE in FECs. *Journal of Further and Higher Education* 37 (1): 38–53.

Cremin, T., P. Burnard, and C. Craft. 2006. Pedagogy and possibility thinking in the early years. *Thinking Skills and Creativity* 1 (2): 108–119.

Crozier, G., D. Reay, J. Clayton, and L. Colliander. 2008. Different strokes for different folks: Diverse students in diverse institutions- experiences of higher education. *Research Papers in Education* 23 (2): 167–177.

Cullimore, S. 2006. Joined-up training: Improving the partnership links between a university PGCE (FE) course and its placement colleges. *Research in Post-compulsory Education* 11 (3): 303–317.

Cunningham, B. 2004. Some have mentoring thrust upon them: The element of choice in mentoring in a PCET environment. *Research in Post-compulsory Education* 9 (2): 271–282.

———. 2007. All the right features: Towards an 'architecture' for mentoring trainee teachers in UK further education colleges. *Journal of Education for Teaching* 33 (1): 83–97.

Daloz, J. 1986. *Effective mentoring and teaching.* San Francisco: Jossey Bass.

Davies, H., and C. Head. 2010. Pedagogical exchange for professional development: Reflections on how collaboration has inspired and empowered a group of early years educators to find new ways of working to improve learning and teaching. *The International Journal of Learning* 17 (9): 339–352.

Delucchi, M., and K. Korgen. 2002. 'We're the customer, we pay the tuition'. Student consumerism among undergraduate sociology majors. *Teaching Sociology* 30 (1): 100–107.

Department for Business Innovation and Skills. 2009. *Higher ambitions: The future of universities in a knowledge economy.* Norwich: HMSO.

———. 2013. *Widening participation in higher education.* London: HMSO.

Department for Education and Skills. 2002. *Success for all.* London: DfES.

———. 2003. *The future of higher education.* Norwich: HMSO.

———. 2004. *Five year strategy for children and learners: Putting people at the heart of public services.* London: The Stationery Office.

———. 2006. *Further education: Raising skills, improving life chances.* Norwich: The Stationery Office.

Department for Education and Skills Standards Unit. 2003. *The future of initial teacher education for the learning and skills sector: An agenda for reform.* London: DfES.

Dewey, J. 1933. *How we think: A restatement of the relation of reflective thinking in the educative process.* New York: Health and Company.

———. 2004. *Democracy and education.* Mineola, N.Y: Dover.

Dimova, Y., and J. Loughran. 2009. Developing a big picture understanding of reflection in pedagogical practice. *Reflective Practice* 10 (2): 205–217.

Dodd-Nufrio, A.T. 2011. Reggio Emilia, Maria Montessori, and John Dewey: Dispelling teachers' misconceptions and understanding theoretical foundations. *Early Childhood Education Journal* 39 (1): 235–237.

Drotner, K., H. Siggaard Jensen, and K. Christian Schroder. 2008. *Informal learning and digital media.* Newcastle: Cambridge Scholars Publishing.

Edwards, D. 1991. Discourse and the development of understanding in the classroom. In *Computers and learning*, ed. O. Boyd-Barrett and E. Scanlon, 186–204. London: Routledge.

Edwards, D., and J. Potter. 1993. Language and causation: A discursive action model of description and attribution. *Psychological Review* 100 (1): 23–41.

Edwards, A., P. Gilroy, and D. Hartley. 2002. *Rethinking teacher education: Collaborative responses to uncertainty.* London: Routledge Falmer.

Edwards, C., L. Gandini, and G. Forman. 2012. *The hundred languages of children: The Reggio Emilia experience in transformation.* Greenwich, CT: Ablex.

Eraut, M. 1994. *Developing professional knowledge and competence.* London: Falmer Press.

———. 2000. Non-formal learning and tacit knowledge in professional work. *British Journal of Educational Psychology* 70 (1): 113–136.

———. 2007. Learning from other people in the workplace. *Oxford Review of Education* 33 (4): 403–422.

Eyles, A., and S. Machin. 2019. The introduction of academy schools to England's education. *Journal of the European Economic Association* 17 (4): 1107–1146.

Feather, D. 2010. A whisper of academic identity: An HE in FE perspective. *Research in Post-compulsory Education* 15 (2): 189–204.

———. 2012. Do lecturers delivering higher education in further education desire to conduct research? *Research in Post-compulsory Education* 17 (3): 335–347.

Fitsimons, E. 2018. *Initial findings from the MCS age 14 sweep.* Swindon: ESRC.

Formby, E., and C. Wolstenholme. 2012. 'If there's going to be a subject that you don't have to do...' Findings from a mapping study of PSHE education in English secondary schools. *Journal of Pastoral Care* 30 (1): 5–18.

Foucault, M. 1971. *Madness and civilisation.* London: Routledge.

———. 1972. *The archaeology of knowledge.* New York: Pantheon.

———. 1977. *Discipline and punish.* London: Allen Lane.

Friedman, M., and R.D. Friedman. 1980. *Free to choose.* London: Penguin.

Frierson, P.R. 2016. Making room for children's autonomy: Maria Montessori's case for seeing children's incapacity for autonomy as an external failing. *Journal of Philosophy of Education* 50 (3): 332–350.

Gadamer, H.-G. 1990. *Warheit und methode.* Tubingen: Mohr Siebeck.

Gane, M. 2000. *Jean Baudrillard: in radical uncertainty.* London: Pluto Press.

Garbutt, G., D. Orrock, and R. Smith. 2013. Culture clash: Mentoring student literacy educators in a marketised and instrumentalist further education policyscape. *Research in Post-compulsory Education* 18 (3): 239–256.

Gee, J.P. 1996. *Social linguistics and literacies.* London: Routledge Falmer.

Geertz, C. 1988. *Works and lives: The anthropologist as author.* Stanford: Stanford University Press.

Gibb, A.A. 1987. Enterprise culture- its meaning and application for education and training. *Journal of European Industrial Training* 11 (2): 38–38.

———. 1997. Enterprise culture and education. Understanding enterprise education and its links with small business, entrepreneurship, and wider educational goals. *International Small Business Journal: Researching Entrepreneurship* 11 (3): 11–34.

Giddens, A. 1979. *Central problems in social theory.* Berkeley: University of California Press.

Giroux, H. 2000. *Impure acts.* London: Taylor and Francis.

———. 2005. *The terror of neo-liberalism: Cultural politics and the promise of democracy.* Boulder, CO: Paradigm Publishers.

Glatter, R. 2012. Persistent preoccupations: The rise and rise of school accountability in England. *Educational Management Administration and Leadership* 40 (5): 559–575.

———. 2013. Academy schools: a flawed system that cannot be sustained. Accessed 21, July, 2016. https://www.theguardian.com/teacher-network/teacher-blog/2013/jan/24/academy-school-system-heading-rocks.

Goffman, E. 1971. *The presentation of the self in everyday life.* London: Pelican Books.

Goldberg, A., M. Russell, and A. Cook. 2003. The effects of computers on students' writing: A meta-analysis from 1992–2002. *Journal of Technology Learning and Assessment* 2 (1): 1–52.

Greany, T., and J. Scott. 2014. *Conflicts of interest in academy sponsorship arrangements. A report for the education select committee.* London: Institute of Education.

Griffiths, V., S. Thompson, and L. Hryniewicz. 2010. Developing a research profile: Mentoring and support for teacher educators. *Professional Development in Education* 36 (1–2): 245–262.

Guilford, J.P. 1967. Creativity: Yesterday, today and tomorrow. *The Journal of Creative Behaviour* 1: 3–14.

Gunter, H. 2011. *Leadership and the reform of education.* Bristol: Policy Press.

Hadley, F., M. Waniganiyake, and W. Shepherd. 2015. Contemporary practice in professional learning and development of early years educators in Australia: Reflections on what works and why. *Professional Development in Education* 41 (2): 187–203.

Hale, J.A. 2008. *A guide to curriculum planning.* Thousand Oaks, CA: Corwin Press.

Hankey, J. 2004. The good, the bad and other considerations: Reflections on mentoring trainee teachers in post-compulsory education. *Research in Post-compulsory Education* 9 (3): 389–400.

Harland, J., and K. Kinder. 2014. Teachers' continuing professional development: Framing a model of outcomes. *Professional Development in Education* 40 (4): 669–682.

Harris, L., and M. Islar. 2013. Neoliberalism nature and changing modalities of environmental governance in contemporary Turkey. In *Global economic crisis and the politics of diversity,* ed. Y. Atasoy, 52–78. London: Palgrave Macmillan.

Harvey, D. 2005. *A brief history of neo-liberalism.* Oxford: Oxford University Press.

Harwood, J., and D. Harwood. 2004. Higher education in further education: Delivering higher education in a further education context: A study of five south west colleges. *Journal of Further and Higher Education* 28 (2): 153–164.

Hassler, B., L. Major, and S. Hennessy. 2015. Tablet use in schools: A critical review of the evidence for learning outcomes. *Journal of Computer Assisted Learning* 32 (2): 139–156.

Hatcher, R. 2011. Local government against local democracy: A case study. In *The state and education policy: The academy programme,* ed. H. Gunter, 39–52. London: Bloomsbury.

Hayek, F. 1976. *Law, legislation and liberty, vol. 2.* London: Routledge and Kegan Paul.

Hayes, D. 2007. *A lecturer's guide to further education: Inside the 'cinderella sector.* Milton Keynes: Open University Press.

Hayes, D., and K. Ecclestone. 2019. *The dangerous rise of therapeutic education.* Oxford: Routledge.

Heidegger, M. 1996. *Being and time*. Albany, N.Y: State University of New York.

Heilbronn, R. 2016. Freedoms and perils: Academy schools in England. *Journal of Philosophy of Education* 50 (3): 306–318.

Hill, R., J. Dunford, N. Parish, S. Rea, and L. Sandals. 2012. *The growth of academy chains: Implications for leaders and leadership*. London: National College for School Leadership.

Hobson, A.J. 2002. Student teachers' perceptions of school-based mentoring in initial teacher training (ITT). *Mentoring & Tutoring* 10 (1): 5–20.

Hudson, B. 2003. *Understanding justice: An introduction to ideas, perspectives and controversies in modern penal history*. Buckinghamshire: Open University Press.

Ilham, N., J.K. Kidd, M.S. Burns, and T. Campbell. 2015. Head start classroom teachers' and assistant teachers' perception of professional development using a LEARN framework. *Professional Development in Education* 41 (2): 344–365.

Ingleby, E. 2010. Robbing Peter to pay Paul: The price of standards-driven education. *Research in Post-compulsory Education* 15 (1): 427–441.

———. 2011. Asclepius or Hippocrates? Differing interpretations of post-compulsory initial teacher training mentoring. *Journal of Vocational Education & Training* 63 (1): 15–25.

———. 2013. Teaching policy and practice: Early years, neoliberalism and communities of practice. *Contemporary social science* 8 (2): 120–129.

———. 2014. Developing reflective practice or judging teaching performance? The implications for mentor training. *Research in post-compulsory education* 19 (1): 18–33.

———. 2015a. The impact of changing policies about technology on the professional development needs of early years educators in England. *Professional Development in Education* 41 (1): 144–158.

———. 2015b. The house that Jack built: Neoliberalism, teaching in higher education and the moral objections. *Teaching in Higher Education* 20 (5): 507–518.

———. 2016. We don't just do what we're told to do! Practitioner perceptions of using ICTs in early years. *International Journal of Early Years Education* 24 (1): 36–48.

———. 2018. Early years educators' perceptions of professional development in England: An exploratory study of policy in practice. *Professional Development in Education* 44 (1): 22–32.

———. 2019. It does more than it says on the tin! Problematising higher education in further education in England. *Studies in Higher Education* 44 (1–2): 20–31.

Ingleby, E., and C. Gibby. 2016. Law and ethics: Problematising the role of the foundation degree and paralegal education in English post-compulsory education. *Research in Post-compulsory Education* 21 (1–2): 151–163.

Ingleby, E., and J. Hunt. 2008. The CPD needs of mentors in post-compulsory initial teacher training in England. *Journal of In-service Education* 34 (1): 61–74.

Ingleby, E., and J.E. Tummons. 2012. Repositioning professionalism: Teachers, mentors, policy and praxis. *Research in Post-compulsory Education* 17 (2): 163–179.

———. 2017. Imitation is not always flattery! The consequences of academy schools in England for further education policy. *Research in Post-compulsory Education* 22 (4): 237–251.

Ingleby, E., and B. Wilford. 2016. Pedagogy with technology in higher education in England. A brave new world? Paper presented at the IPDA conference, 25–26 November, Birmingham, UK.

Ingleby, E., B. Wilford, and C. Hedges. 2019. Teaching with technology and higher education: A brave new world? *Practice: Contemporary Issues in Practitioner Education* 1 (1): 73–87.

Jacobs, G., and M. Murray. 2010. Developing critical understanding by teaching action research to undergraduate psychology students. *Educational Action Research* 18 (3): 319–335.

Jones, R. 1980. Microcomputers: Their uses in primary schools. *Cambridge Journal of Education* 10 (3): 144–153.

Kateb, G. 2011. *Human dignity*. Cambridge, MA: Harvard University Press.

Kauder, P., and W. Fischer. 1999. *Immanuel Kant uber pedagogik: 7 studien*. Baltmannsweiler: Schneider-Verl. Hohengehren.

Kauko, J., and M. Salokangas. 2015. The evaluation and steering of English academy schools through inspection and examinations: National visions and local practices. *British Educational Research Journal* 41 (6): 1108–1124.

Kennedy, A. 2005. Models of CPD: A framework for analysis. *Journal of In-service Education* 31 (2): 235–250.

Kirkup, G., and A. Kirkwood. 2005. Information and communications technologies (ICT) in higher education teaching- a tale of gradualism rather than revolution. *Learning, Media and Technology* 30 (2): 185–199.

Kirkwood, A., and L. Price. 2014. Technology enhanced learning and teaching in higher education: What is 'enhanced' and how do we know? A critical literature review. *Learning, Media and Technology* 39 (1): 6–36.

Krek, J. 2015. Two principles of early moral education: A condition for the law, reflection and autonomy. *Studies in Philosophy and Education* 34: 9–29.

Krippendorp, K. 2004. *Content analysis: An introduction to its methodology*. Thousand Oaks, CA: Sage.

Lane, R.J. 2000. *Jean Baudrillard*. London: Routledge.

Lauder, H., P. Brown, J. Dillabough, and A.H. Halsey. 2006. The prospects for education: Individualisation, globalisation and social change. In *Education globalisation and social change*, ed. H. Lauder, P. Brown, J. Dillabough, and A.H. Halsey, 1–70. Oxford: Oxford University Press.

Lawy, R., and M. Tedder. 2011. Mentoring and individual learning plans: Issues of practice in a period of transition. *Research in Post-compulsory Education* 16 (3): 385–396.

Layen, S. 2015. Do reflections on personal autobiography as captured in narrated life-stories illuminate leadership development in the field of early childhood. *Professional Development in Education* 41 (2): 254–273.

Leask, M., and S. Younie. 2013. National models for continuing professional development: The challenges of twenty first century knowledge management. *Professional Development in Education* 39 (2): 273–287.

Leaton Gray, S.L., and G. Whitty. 2010. Social trajectories or disrupted identities? Changing and competing models of teacher professionalism under new labour. *Cambridge Journal of Education* 40 (1): 5–23.

Li, Z. 2018. *A new approach to Kant*. Singapore: Springer.

Lieberman, J. 2009. Reinventing teacher professional norms and identities: The role of lesson study and learning communities. *Professional Development in Education* 35 (1): 83–99.

Lightfoot, S., and D. Frost. 2015. The professional identity of early years educators in England: Implications for a transformative approach to continuing professional development. *Professional Development in Education* 41 (2): 401–418.

Lillard, A. 2005. *Montessori: The science behind the genius*. Oxford: Oxford University Press.

Lindon, J. 2012. *Reflective practice and early years professionalism*. 2nd ed. London: Hodder Education.

Linklater, H. 2006. Listening to learn: Children playing and talking about the reception year of early years education in the UK. *Early Years* 26 (1): 63–78.

Loughran, J. 2006. *Developing a pedagogy of teacher education: Understanding teaching and learning about teaching*. Abingdon: Routledge.

Löwith, K. 1993. *Marx and Weber*. London: Routledge.

Lucas, N. 2007. Rethinking initial teacher education for further education teachers: From a standards-led to a knowledge-based approach. *Teaching Education* 18 (2): 93–106.

Luckner, A. 2003. Erziehung zur freiheit. Immanuel Kant und die padagogik. *Padagogik* 7–8: 72–76.

Macfarlane, K., and J. Cartmel. 2012. Circles of change revisited: Building leadership, scholarship and professional identity in the children's services sector. *Professional Development in Education* 38 (5): 845–861.

Machin, S., and K. Salvanes. 2010. *Valuing school quality via school choice reform*. London: Centre for the Economics of Education.

Machin, S., and J. Vernoit. 2011. *Changing school autonomy: Academy schools and their introduction to England's education*. London: Centre For The Economics of Education.

Manning, T., and A. Hobson. 2017. Judgemental and developmental mentoring in further education initial teacher education in England: Mentor and mentee perspectives. *Research in Post-compulsory Education* 22 (4): 574–595.

Marklund, L. 2015. Preschool teachers' informal online professional development in relation to educational use of tablets in Swedish preschools. *Professional Development in Education* 41 (2): 236–253.

Marsh, J., G. Brooks, J. Hughes, L. Ritchie, S. Roberts, and K. Wright. 2005. *Digital beginnings: young children's use of popular culture, media and new technologies*. Sheffield: University of Sheffield Literacy Research Centre.

Mathers, S., F. Linksey, J. Seddon, and K. Sylva. 2007. Using quality rating scales for professional development: Experiences from the UK. *International Journal of Early Years Education* 15 (3): 261–2714.

Maynard, T., and J. Furlong. 1993. Learning to teach and models of mentoring. In *Echoes from Freire for a critically engaged pedagogy*, ed. P. Mayo. London: Bloomsbury. 2013.

Mayo, P. 2013. *Echoes from Freire for a critically engaged pedagogy*. London: Bloomsbury.

McCrone, T., C. Southcott, and N. George. 2011. *Governance models in schools: Local government education and children's services*. Slough: NFER.

McIntyre, D., H. Hagger, and M. Wilkin. *Mentoring*, 69–85. London: Kogan Page.

McKie, L., S. Bowlby, and S. Gregory. 2001. Gender, caring and employment in Britain. *Journal of Social Policy* 30 (2): 233–258.

McLean, M., A. Abbas, and P. Ashwin. 2013. A Bernsteinian view of learning and teaching undergraduate sociology-based social science. *Enhancing Learning in the Social Sciences* 5 (2): 32–44.

McLeod, N. 2015. Reflecting on reflection: Improving teachers' readiness to facilitate participatory learning with young children. *Professional Development in Education* 41 (2): 254–273.

McNay, L. 1994. *Foucault: A critical introduction*. Cambridge: Polity Press.

Mercer, N., S. Hennessy, and P. Warwick. 2019. Dialogue, thinking together and digital technology in the classroom: Some educational implications of a continuing line of inquiry. *International Journal of Educational Research* 97: 187–199.

Mezirow, J. 1997. Transformative learning: Theory to practice. In *Transformative learning in action: Insights from practice: New directions for adult and continuing education*, ed. P. Cranton, 5–12. San Francisco, CA: Jossey-Bass.

Minott, M.A. 2010. Reflective teaching as self-directed professional development: Building practical or work-related knowledge. *Professional Development in Education* 36 (2): 325–338.

National Audit Office. 2017. Accessed April 12, 2017. http://www.nao.org.uk.

Nutbrown, C. 2012. *Foundations for quality: The independent review of early education and childcare qualifications*. London: Department for Education.

O'Donnell, M. 2013. *Maria Montessori: A critical introduction to key themes and debates.* London: Continuum.

Ofsted (Office for Standards in Education). 2003. *The initial training of further education teachers in England: A survey.* London: HMSO.

———. 2006. *The initial training of further education teachers: Findings from 2004/05 inspection of courses leading to national awarding body qualifications.* London: Ofsted.

———. 2007. *The initial training of further education teachers.* London: Ofsted.

———. 2008. *The initial training of further education teachers.* London: Ofsted.

Olssen, M., J.A. Codd, and M.A. O'Neill. 2004. *Education policy: Globalisation, citizenship and democracy.* London: Sage.

Papanastasiou, N. 2013. Commercial actors and the governing of education: The case of academy school sponsors in England. *European Educational Research Journal* 12 (4): 447–462.

Parker-Rees, R., C. Leeson, J. Willan, and J. Savage. 2010. *Early childhood studies.* 3rd ed. Exeter: Learning Matters.

Parry, G. 2003. Mass higher education and the English: Where in the colleges? *Higher Education Quarterly* 57 (4): 308–337.

———. 2007. The English experiment. *Journal of University Studies* 35 (1): 95–110.

Parry, G., and A. Thompson. 2002. *Closer by degrees: The past, present and future of higher education in further education colleges.* London: Learning and Skills Development Agency.

Parry, G., C. Callender, P. Scott, and P. Temple. 2012. *Understanding higher education in further education colleges.* London: Department for Business Innovation and Skills, HMSO.

Perry, B., and M. MacDonald. 2015. Educators' expectations and aspirations around young children's mathematical knowledge. *Professional Development in Education* 41 (2): 336–382.

Perryman, J., S. Ball, M. Maguire, and A. Braun. 2011. Life in the pressure cooker-school league tables in English and mathematics teachers' responsibilities in a results driven era. *British Journal of Educational Studies* 59 (2): 179–195.

Peters, R.S. 1963. Reason and habit: The paradox of moral education. In *Moral education in a changing society*, ed. W.R. Niblett, 46–65. London: Faber.

Philippou, S., C. Papademetri-Kachrimani, and L. Louca. 2015. 'The exchange of ideas was mutual, I have to say': Negotiating researcher and teacher 'roles' in an early years educators' professional development programme on inquiry-based mathematics and science learning. *Professional Development in Education* 41 (2): 382–400.

Plowman, L., and C. Stephen. 2005. Children, play and computers in pre-school education. *British Journal of Educational Technology* 36 (2): 145–157.

Posner, G.J. 1989. *Field experience methods of reflective teaching.* New York: Basic Books.

Potter, C.A. 2007. Developments in UK early years policy and practice: Can they improve outcomes for disadvantaged children? *International Journal of Early Years Education* 15 (2): 171–180.

Poulantzas, N. 1978. *State, power, socialism.* London: New Left Books.

Prensky, M. 2001. Digital natives. Digital immigrants part 1. *On the Horizon* 9 (5): 1–6.

Procter, R. 2007. Collaboration, coherence and capacity-building: The role of DSpace in supporting and understanding the TLRP. *Technology, Pedagogy and Education* 16 (3): 269–288.

Purcell, K. 2014. Discourses of aspiration, opportunity and attainment: Promoting and contesting the academy schools programme. *Children's Geographies* 9 (1): 49–61.

Quality Assurance Authority. 2010. *Foundation degree qualification benchmark.* Gloucester: Quality Assurance Agency for Higher Education.

———. 2014. *Subject benchmark statement: Early childhood studies.* Gloucester: Quality Assurance Agency for Higher Education.

Randall, F., and R.S. Downie. 1996. *Palliative care ethics: A good companion (Oxford Medical Publications).* Oxford: Oxford University Press.

Reed, M., and N. Canning. 2010. *Reflective practice in the early years.* London: Sage.

Rowbottom, D.P., and S.J. Aiston. 2006. The myth of 'scientific method' in contemporary educational research. *Journal of Philosophy of Education* 40 (2): 137–156.

Ruhloff, J. 1975. Wie kultiviere ich die freiheit bei dem zwange? *Vierteljahresschrift fur wissenschaftliche padagogik* 51: 2–18.

Sachs, J. 2010. Teacher professional identity: Competing discourses, competing outcomes. *Journal of Education Policy* 16 (2): 149–161.

Salokangas, M., and C. Chapman. 2014. Exploring governance in two chains of academy schools: A comparative case study. *Educational Management Leadership and Administration* 42 (3): 372–386.

Saunders, D.B. 2010. Neoliberal ideology and public education in the United States. *The Journal of Critical Education Policy Studies* 8 (1): 42–77.

Schaffar, B. 2014. Changing the definition of education. On Kant's educational paradox between freedom and restraint. *Studies in Philosophy and Education* 33 (1): 5–21.

Schofield, C., and H. Dismore. 2010. Predictors of retention and achievement of higher education students within a further education context. *Journal of Further and Higher Education* 34 (2): 207–221.

Schön, D.A. 1978. *Educating the reflective practitioner: Toward a new design for teaching.* San Francisco, CA: Jossey-Bass.

Schwandt, T.A. 2005. *A diagnostic of scientifically based research for education.* Malden, MA: Blackwell.

Scott, S. 2010. Pragmatic leadership development in Canada: Investigating a mentoring approach. *Professional Development in Education* 36 (4): 597–621.

Scribner, S., and M. Cole. 1981. *The psychology of literacy.* Cambridge, MA: Harvard University Press.

Selwyn, N. 2011. The place of technology in the conservative-Liberal democrat education agenda: An ambition of absence? *Educational Review* 63 (4): 395–408.

Simmons, R. 2010. Globalisation, neo-liberalism and vocational learning: The case of further education colleges. *Research in Post-compulsory Education* 15 (4): 363–376.

Simpson, D. 2010. Becoming professional? Exploring early years professional status and its implications for workforce reform in England. *Journal of Early Childhood Research* 8 (3): 269–281.

———. 2011. Reform, inequalities of process and the transformative potential of communities of practice in the pre-school sector in England. *British Journal of Sociology of Education* 32 (5): 699–716.

Slaughter, S., and G. Rhodes. 2004. *Academic capitalism and the new economy: Markets states and higher education.* Baltimore, MD: The Johns Hopkins University Press.

Smith, A. 1991. *The wealth of nations.* London: Everyman.

Strathern, M., ed. 2000. *Audit cultures: Anthropological studies in accountability, ethics and the academy.* London: Routledge.

Swap, W., D. Leonard, M. Shields, and L. Abrams. 2001. Using mentoring and storytelling to transfer knowledge in the workplace. *Journal of Management Information Systems* 18 (1): 95–114.

Tedder, M., and R. Lawy. 2009. The pursuit of 'excellence': Mentoring in further education initial teacher training in England. *Journal of Vocational Education and Training* 61 (4): 413–429.

Thatcher, M. 1983. Cited in Hansard House of Commons Parliamentary Questions—March 29, 1983 [40/177–82]. London: Hansard House of Commons.

The Guardian Online. n.d. Accessed November 18, 2020. http://www.guardian.com.uk.

Thomas, L. 2001. Power, assumptions and prescriptions: A critique of widening participation policy-making. *Higher Education Policy* 14 (4): 361–377.

Tickell, C. 2011. *The early years: Foundations for life, health and learning: An independent report on the early years foundation stage to her Majesty's government.* London: Department for Education.

Tigelaar, D., D. Dolmanns, W. Grave, I. Wolfhangen, and C. Vleuten. 2005. Participants' opinions on the usefulness of a teaching portfolio. *Medical Education* 40 (4): 371–378.

Torres, C.A. 1998. *Democracy, education and multiculturalism*. Lanham: Rowman and Littlefield.

———. 2008. *Education and neoliberal globalisation*. New York: Taylor and Francis.

Trim, P. 2001. A review of educational partnership arrangements in further and higher education: Pointers for managers in further education. *Research in Post-compulsory Education* 6 (2): 187–203.

Tummons, J.E. 2011. It sort of feels uncomfortable: Problematising the assessment of reflective practice. *Studies in Higher Education* 36 (4): 471–483.

———. 2014. The textual representation of professionalism: Problematising professional standards for teachers in the UK lifelong learning sector. *Research in Post-compulsory Education* 19 (1): 33–44.

Tummons, J.E., and E. Ingleby. 2012. The problematics of mentoring, and the professional learning of trainee teachers in the English further education sector. *International Journal of Adult Vocational Education and Technology* 3 (1): 29–40.

———. 2014. *An A-Z of the lifelong learning sector*. Maidenhead: Open University Press.

Tummons, J.E., K. Orr, and L. Atkins. 2013. *Teaching higher education courses in further education colleges*. London: SAGE/Learning Matters.

Tymms, P., and C. Merrell. 2007. *Standards and quality in English primary schools over time: The national evidence (primary review survey 4/1)*. Cambridge: University of Cambridge Faculty of Education.

Urban, M. 2008. Dealing with uncertainty: Challenges and possibilities for the early childhood profession. *European Early Childhood Education Research Journal* 16 (2): 135–152.

———. 2009. Strategies for change: rethinking professional development to meet the challenges of diversity in the early years profession. Paper presented at the IPDA conference, 27–28 November, Birmingham, UK.

Van Andel, J., C. Pimentel Botas, and J. Huisman. 2012. The consumption values and empowerment of the student as customer: Taking a rational look inside higher education's 'Pandora's box'. *Higher Education Review* 45 (1): 62–85.

Vanderstraeten, R., and G.J.J. Biesta. 2001. How is education possible? Preliminary investigations for a theory of education. *Educational Philosophy and Theory* 33 (1): 7–21.

Vermunt, J.D. 2016. Keynote address. Paper presented at the IPDA conference, 25–26 November, Stirling, UK.

Waller, T. 2005. *An introduction to early childhood: A multidisciplinary approach*. London: Paul Chapman.

Waters, J., and J. Payler. 2015. The professional development of early years educators- achieving systematic, sustainable and transformative change. *Professional Development in Education* 41 (2): 161–169.

Wenger, E. 1998. *Communities of practice: Learning, meaning and identity.* Cambridge: Cambridge University Press.

Wild, P., and P. King. 1999. Education and IT policy: Virtual policy? In *Education policy and contemporary policy,* ed. J. Demaine, 175–195. Basingstoke: Macmillan Press.

Wilkins, C. 2011. Professionalism and the post-performative teacher: New teachers reflect on autonomy and accountability in the English school system. *Professional Development in Education* 37 (3): 389–409.

Wilkins, A. 2017. Rescaling the local: Multi-academy trusts, private monopoly and statecraft in England. *Educational Administration and History* 49 (2): 171–186.

Willetts, D. 2011. Ron Dearing lecture: universities and social mobility, 17th February, in University of Nottingham, Nottingham.

Williams, J. 2013. *Consuming higher education: Why learning can't be bought.* London: Bloomsbury.

Wilson, A., and B. Wilson. 2011. Pedagogy of the repressed: Research and professionality within HE in FE. *Research in Post-compulsory Education* 16 (4): 465–478.

Winton, P., P. Snyder, and S. Goffin. 2016. Beyond the status-quo: Rethinking professional development for early childhood teachers. In *Handbook of early childhood teacher education,* ed. L. Couse and S. Recchia, 54–68. New York: Routledge.

Woods, A., J. Woods, and H. Gunter. 2007. Academy schools and entrepreneurialism in education. *Journal of Education Policy* 22 (2): 237–259.

Yandell, J., and A. Turvey. 2007. Standards or communities of practice? Competing models of workplace learning and development. *British Educational Research Journal* 33 (4): 533–540.

Yelland, N., and A. Kilderry. 2010. Becoming numerate with information technologies in the twenty-first century. *International Journal of Early Years Education* 18 (2): 91–106.

Young, M. 2006. Further and higher education: Seamless or differentiated future? *Journal of Further and Higher Education* 30 (1): 1–10.

INDEX

© The Author(s), under exclusive license to Springer Nature Switzerland AG 2021
E. Ingleby, *Neoliberalism Across Education*, Palgrave Studies on Global Policy and Critical Futures in Education,
https://doi.org/10.1007/978-3-030-73962-1

Printed in Great Britain
by Amazon